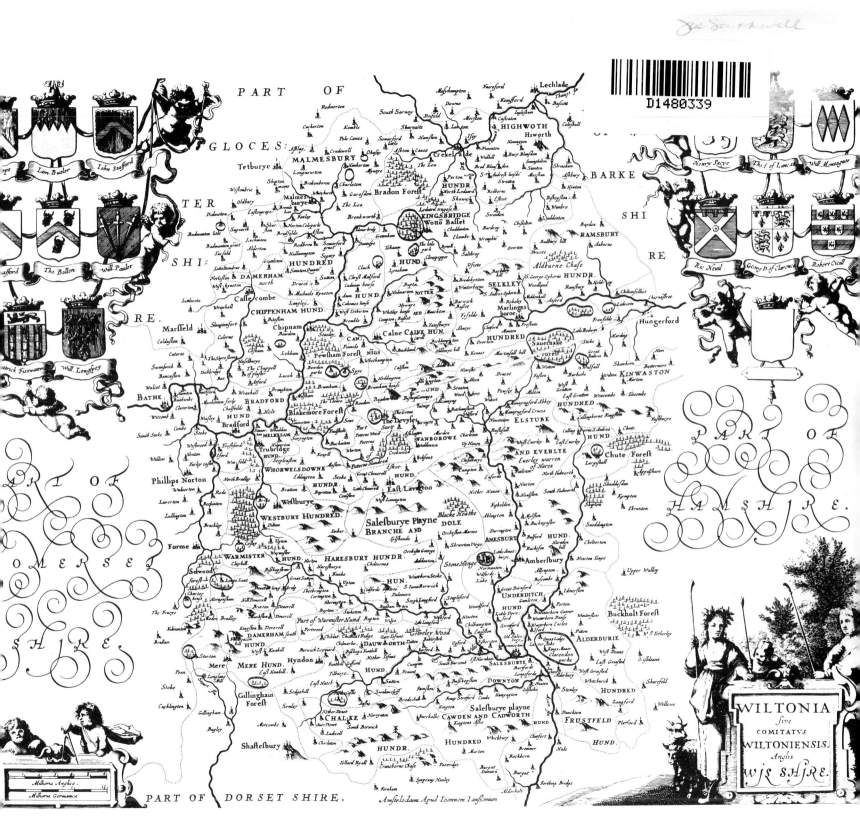

WILTONIA
sive
COMITATVS
WILTONIENSIS.
Anglis
WIL SHIRE.

PART OF DORSET SHIRE.

Amstelodami Apud Ioannem Ianssonium

WESSEX *Images*

The Square, Corfe Castle

WESSEX *Images*

—*JOHN CHANDLER*—

ALAN SUTTON

Wiltshire
COUNTY COUNCIL
LIBRARY & MUSEUM SERVICE

First published in the United Kingdom in 1990 by
Alan Sutton Publishing · Phoenix Mill · Far Thrupp · Stroud · Gloucestershire

First published in the United States of America in 1991 by
Alan Sutton Publishing Inc. Wolfeboro Falls · NH 03896–0848

British Library Cataloguing in Publication Data

Chandler, John H. (John Howard), 1951–
Wessex images.
1. Wessex. Rural regions. Social life, history
I. Title
942.3

ISBN 0–86299–739–9

Library of Congress Cataloging in Publication Data applied for

Endpapers: Jan Jansson's maps of Wiltshire and Dorset, 1651

Front Cover Photograph: Gold Hill, Shaftesbury (*Tim Hawkins*)

Back Cover Photograph: Marlborough Downs, near Rockley (*Michael Dunsby*)

Previous Page Photograph: Burton Bradstock

Photoset Bembo 11/13.
Typesetting and origination by Alan Sutton Publishing Limited.
Colour and duotones by Spa Graphics Limited, Cheltenham.
Printed in Great Britain by the Guernsey Press Company Limited.

Introduction

What is Wessex? Depending on our interests and our mood it may conjure up King Alfred and his Saxon kingdom, or the tragic heroes and heroines of Thomas Hardy, or more prosaically – if we live there – the authority to whom we pay our water rates. 'Wessex' is a flexible word, and it can be used to describe a very large area; but for the purposes of this book it simply means the two ancient counties of Dorset and Wiltshire.

Despite this restriction our Wessex is still a large place, home to more than a million people, and stretching some eighty miles from the cliffs of Lyme Regis to the Thames Valley near Cricklade. If there were a single image of this Wessex it would be a scene of chalk downland, with sheep perhaps, and in the distance a cluster of roofs and a church tower set among cornfields in a valley. But that is only one of many images – dairy farms, heathlands, coastlines and busy towns – to be found in this region, and in this book. The images come as pictures, ancient and modern, and also in verbal form, portraits of Wessex scenery and Wessex life, as seen by visitors and residents over the years, from Alfred to Hardy.

'I cannot understand time,' confesses one of our contributors, '. . . the years, the centuries, the cycles are absolutely nothing.' In a sense he is right. Much of the Wessex landscape, of hills and vales, cliffs and rivers, seemed then – and seems now – to be wrapped in an air of timelessness; although a century later we are coming to realize how fragile that air of timelessness may be. But those hills and rivers, whatever we may have done to them, remain the benchmarks of our history – kings and pilgrims, vicars, thieves and scholars have had to climb them and cross over them, and just occasionally they have recorded what they saw and what they felt.

In this book the inhibitions imposed by time can be suspended. It is the spirit of place, not time, that is paramount. The people whose views have found their way between the covers of this book did not, for the most part, know each other – they are drawn from different epochs, different social strata, different worlds almost. But there exists between them a common bond, which binds us too when we travel around Wessex. Today's tourist, happily photographing Dorchester, will not meet Thomas Hardy and William Barnes in the flesh; and they in turn never met Celia Fiennes or Daniel Defoe, William Whiteway or John Leland. But the streets of Dorcester – the places of Wessex – have known them all.

Perhaps it is a pity that John Aubrey never met Francis Kilvert, and Edward Thomas could not be introduced to William Gilpin. What would Jane Austen have thought of Deborah Primrose? What would Geoffrey of Monmouth have thought of the ticket-barrier at Stonehenge? And how would William Cobbett have coped with the M4? We shall never know. But through their words we can at least find out what they thought about the Wessex of their day, and compare their images with our own.

Westbury White Horse

WESSEX *Images*

Our sequence begins when Wessex meant the kingdom of Wessex, which stretched, at its greatest extent, from Cornwall to Kent. In 878 its most famous king, Alfred, was gathering his forces to fight off a Viking army camped at Chippenham which threatened to annihilate his kingdom. Alfred had a sympathetic biographer, teacher and friend, a Welsh bishop named Asser, and in this extract, fresh from recounting the episode of the cakes, Asser describes the fateful battle on Salisbury Plain, contemptuously referring to the Vikings simply as 'pagans'.

In the same year, after Easter, King Alfred, with a few followers, made for himself a stronghold in a place called Athelney, and from thence sallied with his vassals and the nobles of Somersetshire, to make frequent assaults upon the pagans. Also, in the seventh week after Easter, he rode to the stone of Egbert, which is in the eastern part of the wood which is called Selwood, which means in Latin *silva magna*, the Great Wood, but in British *coit-mawr*. Here he was met by all the neighbouring folk of Somersetshire, and Wiltshire, and Hampshire, who had not, for fear of the pagans, fled beyond the sea; and when they saw the king alive after such great tribulation, they received him, as he deserved, with joy and acclamations, and encamped there for one night. When the following day dawned, the king struck his camp, and went to Acglea, where he encamped for one night. The next morning he removed to Ethandun, and there fought bravely and perseveringly against all the army of the pagans, whom, with the divine help, he defeated with great slaughter, and pursued them flying to their fortification. Immediately he slew all the men, and carried off all the booty that he could find outside the fortress, which he immediately lay siege to with all his army; and when he had been there fourteen days, the pagans, driven by famine, cold, fear, and last of all by despair, asked for peace, on the condition that they should give the king as many hostages as he pleased, but should receive none of him in return, in which form they had never before made a treaty with anyone. The king, hearing that, took pity upon them, and received such hostages as he chose; after which the pagans swore, moreover, that they would immediately leave the kingdom; and their king, Guthrum, promised to embrace Christianity, and receive baptism at King Alfred's hands. All of which articles he and his men fulfilled as they had promised.

Asser was writing soon after the events he describes, and in general his account is thought to be trustworthy. Not so our next informant, whose HISTORY OF THE KINGS OF BRITAIN has been taken with a very large pinch of salt ever since he wrote it in the twelfth century. His name, he tells us (in Latin), was Galfridus Monumotensis, or Geoffrey of Monmouth, and his 'history' is an entertaining blend of legend, half-truth and medieval fantasy. But it is as a work of literature that Geoffrey's book has endured the centuries, and its strange tales, in which (according to one editor) 'history keeps peeping through the fiction', have been repeatedly borrowed and half-believed.

We left Alfred flushed with success after his victory at Ethandun. The site of the battle is believed to be on the downs above Westbury, near the village now called Edington. To commemorate that victory, there is a tradition that a horse was cut

Salisbury Plain

into the chalk hillside, a forerunner of the present Westbury White Horse which was made in 1778, nine hundred years later. Alfred's horse probably has no more basis in fact, however, than the following account, which is Geoffrey's attempt to explain Stonehenge in a similar way, as a monument to an earlier, shadowy encounter, at which British envoys were treacherously killed by the Saxons. His story begins when Aurelius, the British king, visits the scene of the massacre on the downs near Amesbury, 'the cloister of Ambrius'.

At this place was a convent which maintained three hundred brethren, situated on the mountain of Ambrius, who, as is reported, had been the founder of it. The sight of the place where the dead lay made the king, who was of a compassionate temper, shed tears, and at last contemplate what kind of monument to erect upon it. For he thought something ought to be done to perpetuate the memory of that piece of ground, which was honoured with the bodies of so many noble patriots, who died for their country.

For this purpose he summoned together several carpenters and masons, and commanded them to employ the utmost of their art, in contriving some new structure, for a lasting monument to those great men. But when they, in diffidence of their own skill, refused to undertake it, Tremorinus, archbishop of the City of Legions, went to the king, and said, 'If any one living is able to execute your commands, Merlin, the prophet of Vortigern, is the man. In my opinion there is not in all your kingdom a person of a brighter genius, either in predicting future events, or in mechanical contrivances. Order him to come to you, and exercise his skill in the work which you design.' Whereupon Aurelius, after he had asked a great many questions concerning him, despatched several messengers into the country to find him out, and bring him to him. After passing through several provinces, they found him in the country of the Gewissei, at the spring of Galabes, which he frequently resorted to. As soon as they had delivered their message to him, they conducted him to the king, who received him with joy. . . .

'If you are desirous,' said Merlin, 'to honour the burying-place of these men with an everlasting monument, send for the Giant's Dance, which is in Killaurus, a mountain in Ireland. For there is a structure of stones there, which none of this age could raise, without a profound knowledge of the mechanical arts. They are stones of a vast magnitude, and wonderful quality; and if they can be placed here, as they are there, round this spot of ground, they will stand for ever.'

At these words of Merlin, Aurelius burst into laughter, and said, 'How is it possible to remove such vast stones from so distant a country, as if Britain was not furnished with stones fit for the work?' Merlin replied, 'I entreat your majesty to forbear vain laughter; for what I say is without vanity. They are mystical stones, and of a medicinal virtue. The giants of old brought them from the farthest coast of Africa, and placed them in Ireland, while they inhabited that country. Their design in this was to make baths beneath them, for use when they should be taken with any illness. For their method was to wash the stones, and put those who were sick into the water, which infallibly cured them. With the like success they cured wounds also, adding only the application of some herbs. There is not a stone there which has not some healing virtue.'

When the Britons heard this, they resolved to send for the stones, and to make war upon the people of Ireland if they should offer to detain them. And to accomplish this business, they made choice of Uther Pendragon, who was to be attended with fifteen thousand men. They chose also Merlin himself, by whose direction the whole affair was to be managed. A fleet being therefore got ready, they set sail, and with a fair wind arrived in Ireland.

At that time Gillomanius, a youth of wonderful valour, reigned in Ireland; who, upon the news of the arrival of the Britons in his kingdom, levied a vast army, and marched out against them. And when he had learned the occasion of their coming, he smiled, and said to those about him, 'No wonder a cowardly race of people were able to make so great a devastation in the island of Britain, when the Britons are such brutes and fools. Was ever the like folly heard of? What – are the stones of Ireland better than those of Britain, that our kingdom must be put to this disturbance for them? To arms, soldiers, and defend your country; while I have life they shall not take from us the least stone of the Giant's Dance.' Uther, seeing them prepared for a battle, attacked them; and it was not long before the Britons had the advantage, who, having dispersed and killed the Irish, forced Gillomanius to flee.

After the victory they went to the mountain of Killaurus, and arrived at the structure of stones, the sight of which filled them with both joy and admiration. And while they were all standing around them, Merlin came up to them and said, 'Now try your forces, young men, and see whether strength or art can do the most towards taking down these stones.' At this word they all set to their engines with one accord, and attempted the removing of the Giant's Dance. Some prepared cables, others small ropes, others ladders for the work, but all to no purpose. Merlin laughed at their vain efforts, and then began his own contrivances. When he had placed in order the engines that were necessary, he took down the stones with an incredible facility, and gave directions for carrying them to the ships, and placing them therein. This done, they with joy set sail again, to return to Britain; where they arrived with a fair wind, and repaired to the burying-place with the stones.

When Aurelius had notice of it, he sent messengers to all parts of Britain, to summon the clergy and people together to the mount of Ambrius, in order to celebrate with joy and honour the erection of the monument. Upon this summons appeared the bishops, abbots, and people of all other orders and qualities; and upon the day and place appointed for their general meeting, Aurelius wore his crown upon his head, and with royal pomp celebrated the feast of Pentecost, the solemnity whereof he continued the three following days. In the meantime, all places of honour that were vacant, he bestowed upon his domestics as rewards for their good services. . . . As soon as he had settled these and other affairs in the kingdom, he ordered Merlin to set up the stones brought over from Ireland, about the sepulchre; which he accordingly did, and placed them in the same manner as they had been in the mountain of Killaurus, and thereby gave a manifest proof of the prevalence of art above strength.

Whatever its origin, Geoffrey's version of this story illustrates two features of many similar medieval tales, an attempt to impress the hearer with the antiquity or importance of the place in question, and an attempt to explain how something – whatever it

may be — came about. On the second point Geoffrey is rather shaky — he clearly had no idea how Stonehenge could have been erected, and so, in time-honoured tradition, explained it as the work of giants and a magician.

Often such legends were connected with great churches and monasteries, and the holy men and women who founded them. Such places were objects of veneration by pilgrims, who, like any tourists, asked questions and demanded impressive explanations. Here are three short passages in this genre. The first is a translation by a seventeenth-century Benedictine monk, Jerome Porter, of a collection of saints' lives made around the time of the Norman conquest by one Goscelin. It relates to Cerne Abbas, and would strike a chord with any footsore pilgrim.

St Augustine, coming into the countie of Dorsett all-waies announcing Christ's holy Ghospell, he arrived at a village where the wicked people not only refused to obey his doctrine, but very impiously and opprobriously beat him and his fellowes out of their village and in mockerie fastened Fish-tayles at their backs: which became a new purchase of eternall glory to the Saincts, but a perpetuall ignominie to the doers. For it is reported that all that generation had that given them by nature which soe contemptibly they fastened on the backs of these holy men. And Saint Augustine having left these wicked people to carrie the markes of their owne shame, and travelled with his holy companie about five miles further through

Devil's Den, Preshute

desert and uninhabited places, being cruelly oppressed with the three familiar discomodities of travellers, hunger, thirst, and wearines, he that sate upon the fountaine wearied with his journey, Christ Jesus, voutchsafed to appear visibly unto him with words of heavenly comfort and encouragement. Then the holy man, being refreshed with the sweet fountaine of eternall life, fell presently uppon his knees and adored the place of Christ's footsteps, and striking his staffe into the ground there straight sprung forth a cleere fountaine of cristall streames, in which all his fellowes quenched the extremitie of their thirst and gave infinite thankes to Allmightie God who had voutchsafed to helpe them in that necessitie.

And the same place was afterwards called Cernel, a name composed of Latine and Hebrew, for Cerno in Latine signifies to see, and El in Hebrew signifies God; because there our holy apostle Augustine was honoured with the cleere vision of him that is true God and man. Moreover upon the same fountaine in memorie hereof a chappell was built dedicated to our Saviour, which, togeather with the fountaine, my Authour had seen; and the water cured manie diseases.

Afterwards one Egelward, a rich man, founded a fayre monastery of Benedictine monks in the same place, dedicated to Saint Peter the Apostle, which was called the monastery of Cernel and dured to the last fatall destruction of Abbeies in the unfortunate raigne of Henry the eight.

The second passage, which seems to contain more than a grain of truth, describes the founding of Malmesbury Abbey, and was almost certainly written down by one of the monks in that seat of medieval learning, probably during the 1360s.

In Ireland there was a monk named Meildulf, who was so harassed by thieves and robbers in his own country that he could barely make a living. Knowing that he could not stay there much longer he made his escape, took to the road and came to England. He travelled around the country, wondering where God would choose for him, and eventually made his home beneath the castle of Bladon, which in the Saxon tongue was called Ingelbourne-castel. This castle had been built by a British king, the 18th after Brutus, whose name was Dunwallo Molmuncius, in the year 642 BC. Once there had been a city there, but this had been almost completely destroyed by the foreigners; the castle defences remained, and for a long time after the birth of Christ continued to stand with no dwellings nearby. The king's dwelling and premises, both in the pagan and Christian periods, was at Kairdureburgh, which is now known as Brukeburgh, or, as some call it, Brokenbern. Now Meildulf the hermit chose to make his hermitage beneath the castle, and was granted permission by the castellan, because very few people ever went there. But because the requirements for life were in short supply, he collected a group of students around him and formed a school, so that he could make a living from their generosity. His students quickly made progress, and the school grew into a small community. Aldhelm was one of those inspired by their example and fellowship, and added the liberal arts to the fullness of his knowledge; but to reach the heart of the subject he went to Canterbury, and there studied at the feet of Adrian the philosopher, who later became archbishop. After he had studied there for a while he returned to Malmesbury, and took the tonsure as a monk in the company of Meildulf and his disciples.

Our third dip into the world of the medieval pilgrim takes us back to Geoffrey's 'cloister of Ambrius'. Amesbury Priory had once boasted the relics of Saint Melor, an obscure Breton martyr. But by the fourteenth century the relics, and the buildings which once had housed them, were gone, and so a rather tall story was needed to explain their absence to perhaps disgruntled visitors. The legend was included in a collection by John Capgrave, a fifteenth-century friar.

Many years later foreign preachers were carrying about the reliquary containing the remains of Saint Melor, and after wandering through the countryside in connection with their duties they eventually arrived at Amesbury, and placed the relics of the saint on the altar. When they had completed their business they wanted to take them away again, but the relics stuck fast to the altar like a magnet, and no way could be found to move them, so the abbess paid the preachers a large sum of money and they went away in great sorrow and distress. Then some children of wickedness broke into Amesbury church at night and took Saint Melor's reliquary away with them, and when they had stripped off the gold and silver leaf they threw the box containing the relics into a cave. But a certain priest, when he arose in the morning, saw a radiant shaft of light falling from heaven onto this cave; he went to the place, found the reliquary, and took it back to the church. Then Saint Melor himself appeared to the priest one night, and said, 'Godric, rise with all haste! The vault of the church roof is shaking and splitting, and the whole structure is about to collapse.' The vision of the saint repeated the same warning on the following night, and on the third night said, 'Godric, rise immediately! Fetch up the images and altar furniture and remove them as quickly as you can. Grave danger stalks within your gates.' As soon as the priest had made his exit the whole roof collapsed behind him, flattening the church.

Whether such stories were believed by the fifteenth-century traveller is a matter for conjecture. William Worcestre, who as steward to Sir John Fastolf of Castle Combe travelled frequently around England, took a keen interest in what he saw and was told. Sometimes he could be gullible, or fall victim to misinformation and misunderstanding. But his diary and topographical writings are nevertheless of great interest, and foreshadow the spirit of enquiry that was to come. First, here is a straightforward entry from his diary.

Sunday 30 August [1478] I spent half the day before noon at Salisbury, and on the same day attended Saint Edith's mass at Wilton Abbey. That same Sunday I reached the village of Cheverell two miles this side of the Vyes [Devizes], where a man called Philip Pure put me up for the night with courtesy. Next day, Monday 31 August, I rode through the Vyes and Yatesbury, and then to the manor of Crofton [Corton], once called Katermayns, in Hilmarton parish, where I did business for Sir Thomas Danvers. Afterwards I rode via Stanley Abbey and Chippenham to arrive at Castle Combe.

Worcestre took great interest in rivers – understandably, since an unbridged river must often have caused busy travellers like him annoyance and a frustrating detour – but without a reliable map the subject could be very confusing.

The source of Avon water is called Mayledun. The first spring is at Calstone, from a hill called the Oldbury in the dale, and it flows through Calne. Another spring, called Panwell, begins at Cherhill two miles beyond Calne and to the north of Calstone; it flows through Calne, meeting the other water at Quemerford near Calne. A third stream, the Marden, rises at a spring called Kellaways or Avon. [Here Worcestre has become confused and deletes a few words.] The Avon rises three miles from West Malmesbury [Westport] at Sherston and flows through Malmesbury, Somerford, Dauntsey, Seagry, Christian Malford, and Kellaways, then joins these other streams a mile from Chippenham, and flows on through Lacock, Melksham, Bath, Keynsham and Bristol. . . .

Castle Combe water rises at Kington under Coldown Hill, which is 1½ miles west of Castle Combe towards Bristol. There is another source of the same water which rises in Littleton Drew lordship a mile from Castle Combe. They meet at Hachpole, flow through Castle Combe to the stream at Ford, and thence to Slaughterford and Box, joining the Avon to the east of Bath.

A stream which at Calne is called Avon rises about six miles beyond Calne, flows through Bradenstoke seven miles away, then through Chippenham and the cities of Bath and Bristol.

A stream at Cherhill hill five miles this side of Marlborough flows through Marlborough, Hungerford, Acham and Newbury, then through Reading, Henley, Maidenhead, etc. . . .

The Salisbury water has one of its sources near Frome Selwood; this is called the Bourne. Another stream originates near the village of Marlford and runs through Collingbourne and Amesbury Abbey, to the north of Salisbury. Another begins on the south side of Salisbury at —— [left blank] and issues into the sea at Christchurch near Southampton. The source of the larger river which flows under Stockbridge bridge is around Reading, and it runs near Andover, Stockbridge and Romsey.

But no, that must be wrong! Try again.

River Kennet, Axford

Harnham Bridge, Salisbury

The several streams running through Salisbury: One of Salisbury's streams rises at Frome Selwood and is called the Bourne. It goes through Warminster and Heytesbury and falls on the west side of —— [left blank]. A second stream begins around the village of Theale near Reading, and goes via Collingbourne, Amesbury Abbey and Old Sarum. Another begins near Andover, goes through Stockbridge and Romsey, and flows into the sea at Southampton, but it does not go through Salisbury. Another rises in the area of the town and monastery of Wilton (south-west of Salisbury), and passes right through the city of Salisbury leaving it on the south side. Then it flows into Romsey water and goes through —— [left blank] but reaches the sea at Christchurch harbour between Southampton and Portland. The several streams join at the southern end of Salisbury upstream from a bridge of six arches called —— [left blank] and run together as far as Shaftesbury, eighteen miles further on, before reaching the sea at Christchurch harbour or at the place called —— [left blank].

Still not right, but Worcestre gives up and moves on to something else. Clearly he was relying on what others had told him, or on guesswork. He surely cannot ever have travelled from Salisbury up the Ebble valley or over Whitesheet to Shaftesbury set on its hill, or he would not have believed that any river could take such a course. Indeed from his writings it seems that he barely ventured into Dorset at all.

Worcestre wrote in Latin, in common with all the authors quoted so far. But as the Middle Ages drew to a close, so the first descriptions of England in English began to appear. John Leland was born in about 1503, some twenty-five years after Worcestre's failure to unravel the drainage pattern of southern England, and he proved to be an altogether more observant, discriminating, and informative traveller. After a remarkably thorough education – at London, Cambridge, Oxford and Paris – he was employed by Henry VIII to rescue for the royal library important books and manuscripts from the collections then being broken up as a result of the dissolution of the monasteries.

His travels took him the length and breadth of England, and into Wales, in the course of about eight years (1535–43), but in 1547 he became insane, and he died in 1552. His ITINERARY remained in manuscript for over 150 years, but since its first publication, between 1710 and 1712, it has provided local historians with a rich quarry of pithy and picturesque quotations about their chosen place, as seen through the quizzical eye of Henry VIII's topographer.

Here we accompany Leland as he makes his way on horseback from the Devon border across west Dorset to Weymouth and Portland (trajectus, incidentally, means a passage or crossing).

From Axmouth to Lime a 4. miles by meatly good ground but no plenty of wood. Lime is a praty market toun set in the rootes of an high rokky hille down to the hard shore. This town hath good shippes, and usith fisshing and marchauntice. Merchauntes of Morleys in Britaine much haunt this town. Ther cummith a shalow brooke from the hilles about a 3. miles of by north, and cummith fleting on great stone thorough a stone bridge in the botom. The tounes men commenely caul this water the Buddel. One Borowgh a marchaunt man in time of minde buildid a fair house in Lime, having a goodly towr at the entery of it. . . .

Britport, of sum written Bruteport, is a fair larg town, and the chief streat of it lyith in lenght from west to est. Ther crosse a nother fair strete in midle of it into the south. At the north ende of this streate is a chapelle of S. Andreas, wher sum say that the paroch chirch was yn old tyme. The paroch chirch of the town is now stonding in the south end of this streate. . . . Ther was in sight or ever I cam over the ryver into Britport a Lazar House: and not far of a chapelle of S. Magdalene in the which is a cantuarie foundid. And over the bridge a litle by west in the town is a chapelle of S. John. Ther is also a chapelle in the town of S. Michael. The town longgith to the king and hath privilege for a market and 2. bailives. From Britport to the north west point of the Chisil renning from Portland

Portland

Limpley Stoke

Chesil, looking east from Bridport

thither about a 5. miles by shore somewhat baying. . . .

I rode from Britport 3. miles to Netherbyri, and then a mile farther to Bemistre. The ground al this way is in an exceding good and almost the best vain of ground for corne, and pasture, and wood, that is in al Dorsetshire. I rode from Bemistre a mile to the toppe of an high hille, and ther I left not far of on the lift hande northworde Ax Knolle, wher Ax ryver risith that goith to Axmouth. Then I rode a mile farther by corn, pasture and wood. And after a 3. miles most by morisch but good pasture ground for brede of catelle onto Evershot, a right homble and poore

market toun. And so a mile to Milbyri by very good ground. Mr. Strangeguayse hath now a late much buildid at Mylbyri, *lapide quadrato*, avauncing the inner part of the house with a loftie and fresch tower. . . . Ther is a fair park hard by the maner place of Milbyri. And yn this park is a pond, out of the wich issuith a broketh that with the course of a right few miles goith into Ivelle ryver. The Stranguaise cam to this lordship by purchace.

From Milbyri up the hille about a mile by frutefulle and meatly welle woddid ground. Then a vi. miles stille by champaine ground on an high rigge, wher in sight was little

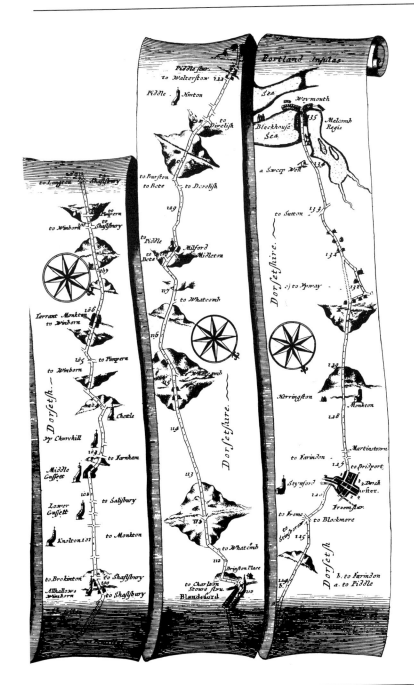

corn and no wood, but al about great flokkes of shepe, from whom al the ground therabout is very propice. Here at the end of the rigge or I descendid I markid to brookes going to Fraw or Frome ryver. . . . Thens I passid down the hille to Frome toun a praty husband town a mile of, and so I passid at the tounes end over a bridge of 3. arches stonding on Frome water. . . . From Frome to Uphil al by hilly ground, baren of wood but exceding good for shepe a 4. miles. At this Uphil on the right hond as I cam is the very hedde of Way ryver, that of sum ys caullid Wile. Heere I cam into the way that ledith from Dorchester to Waymouth 3. good miles distant from this place, by al the which way I rode as yn a base level ground. Dorchester is 8. miles from Waymouth.

Ther is a townlet on the hither side of the haven of Waymouth caullid Miltoun beyng privilegid and having a mair. This toun, as it is evidently seene, hathe beene far bigger than it is now. The cause of this is layid onto the French-men that yn tymes of warre rasid this towne for lak of defence. For so many houses as be yn the town they be welle and strongly buildid of stone. Ther is a chapelle of ease in Milton. The paroch chirch is a mile of: a manifest token that Milton is no very old town. Ther was a fair house of Freres in the est part of the town: and the chief house of the Rogers in Dorsetshir was founder and patrone of it. Milton stondith as a peninsula by reason of the water of the haven that a litle above the toun spreddith abrode and makith a bay: and by the bay of the mayne se that gulfith in on the other side.

The tounlet of Waymouth lyith strait agayn Milton on the other side of the haven, and at this place the water of the haven is but of a smaul brede: and the *trajectus* is by a bote and a rope bent over the haven; so that yn the fery boote they use no ores. Waigmouth hath certein libertees and privileges, but ther is no mair yn it. Ther is a kay and warf for shippes. By this toun on an hille is a chapelle of ease. The paroche chirch is a mile of. The ryver of Way or Wile risith not 4 miles ful above Waymouth by north west

Portland Bill

The Purbeck Hills

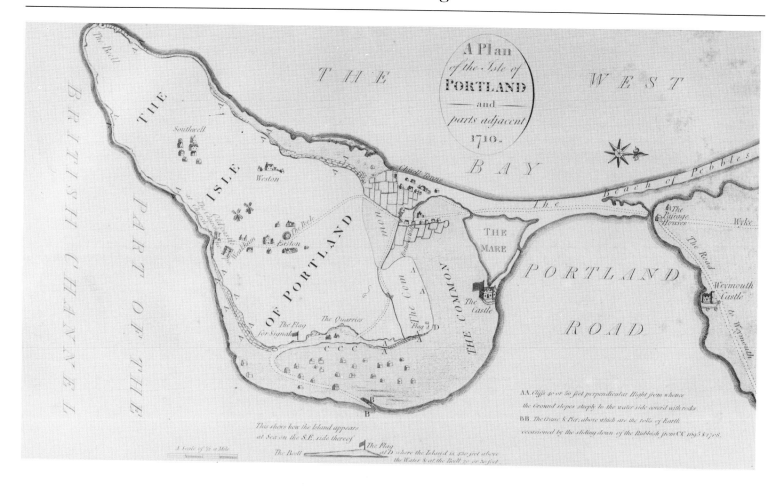

at Uphil in the side of a great hille. The se ebbith and flowith up aboute a 2. miles beyond Weymouth. Ther is a little barre of sand at the haven mouth.

Ther rennith up by the right hond of the haven a great arme of the se: and scant a mile above the haven mouth on the shore of this arme is a right goodly and warlyke castel made, having one open barbicane. This arme rennith up farther a mile as in a bay to a point of land wher a *trajectus* is into Portland by a long causey of pible and sand. This arme goith up from the strait of the trajectus and is of a good bredth, and so se lyke goith' up to Abbates-Byri about a vii. miles of, where is a litle fresch resorting to the se. . . .

The nature of this bank of Chisil is such that as often as the wind blowith strene at south est so often the se betith it and losith the bank and sokith thorough it; so that if this winde might most continually blow there this bank should sone be beten away and the se fully enter and devide Portland, making it an isle, as surely in tymes past it hath beene as far as I can by any conjecture gather. But as much

as the south est wind dooth bete and breke of this Chisille bank, so much doth the north west wynd again socor, strengith and augmentith it.

On the farther point of the *trajectus* into Porteland cumming from Waymouth is a point of land like a causey al of pible and sand cast up by rages of the se, wheron I went scant a mile to the lowest part of the rotes of the high ground of Portland, wher a late a right strong and magnificent castel is buildid. And from this castelle to the very south est point of the Chisil is but a litle way: and the arme of the se that goith up to Abbates-Byri gulfith in bytwixt the south est point of the Chisil and the castelle.

William Camden, scarcely a year old when mad Leland died, was the next to take up the mantle of topographical research. In 1586 *he published* BRITANNIA, *a systematic description, county by county, of places and antiquities. This monument of Elizabethan scholarship was consulted, quoted, or corrected by everyone who followed in Camden's wake for more than two centuries. John Aubrey, whom we shall meet soon, recorded the antiquary at work: 'When my grandfather went to schoole at Yatton-Keynell Mr. Camden came to see the church, and particularly tooke notice of a little painted-glasse-windowe in the chancell, which (ever since my remembrance) haz been walled-up, to save the parson the chardge of glazing it.'*

Here are Camden's observations on Purbeck – and incidentally on mothers-in-law.

From thence the shore lies strait along by the Island Purbeck (as they call it,) which is full of heath, woods, and

Corfe

A Prospect of the Town of POOLE from the West End of BRUNCKSEY ISLAND.

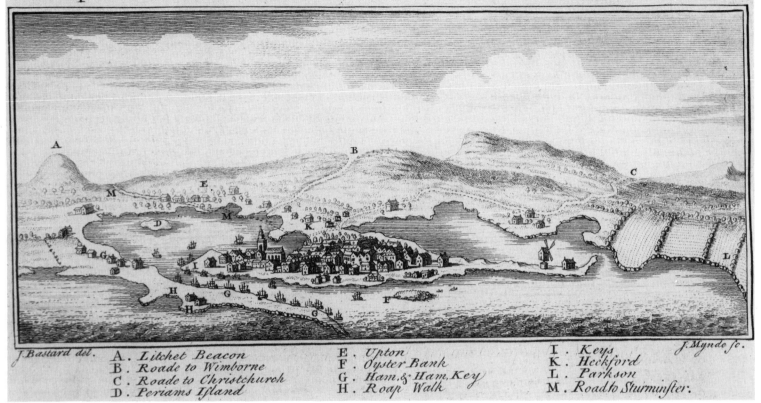

J. Bastard del.

J. Mynde sc.

A . Litchet Beacon
B . Roade to Wimborne
C . Roade to Christchurch
D . Periams Island

E . Upton
F . Oyster Bank
G . Ham & Ham Key
H . Roap Walk

I . Keys
K . Heckford
L . Parkson
M . Road to Sturminster.

forests, well stock'd with Fallow-deer and stags; and containing under ground, here and there, some veins of marble. In the middle of it stood formerly an old Castle called Corffe, a very ancient ruin, but at last fallen quite to shatters, which nevertheless is a notable memorial of the spite of Mothers-in-law. For Aelfrith (that she might make way for her own son Etheldred to the Throne) when her son-in-law Edward King of England made her a visit here as he came from hunting, set some Ruffians upon him, who slew him; whilst his impious step-mother glutted her eyes with the Scene of his murder. Which impiety she afterwards, by a late repentance, us'd her utmost endeav-

ours to expiate, assuming the habit of a Nun, and building Religious houses. This Purbeck is call'd an Island, though it be but a Peninsula; being every way wash'd by the sea, but westward; for towards the East, the banks of the sea wind very much inward, which having a strait and narrow inlet or passage, (opposite to which within is an Island with a blockhouse call'd Brenksey,) widens and expands it self to a bay of a great breadth. To the north of which, in a peninsula hard by, is Poole, a small town, so situated that the waters surround it every way but northward, where 'tis joyn'd to the continent, and has only one gate. It is not unlikely that it took its name from that bay below it, which in a calm seems as it were a standing water, and such as we, in our Language, call a Pool. This, in the last age, was improv'd from a Sedge-plat with a few Fishermens huts, to a well frequented market-town, and grew very wealthy, being adorn'd with fair buildings. K. Hen. 6. by Act of Parliament transferr'd the franchises of the port of Melcombe, which he had disfranchis'd, to this place; and gave leave to the Mayor to enclose it with walls, which were afterwards begun at the haven by that Rich. 3. who deservedly bears the character of one of the worst of men, and best of Kings. But from that time (by I know not what ill destiny, or rather negligence of the towns-men) it has been decaying; so that now the houses, for want of inhabitants, are quite out of repair.

Camden's erudition, especially after the original Latin version had been translated into English with the author's cooperation in 1610, opened the way for variations on the topographer's theme. None is more startling, to the modern ear, than a work which was published in 1612 with the title POLY-OLBION (Greek for 'an abundance of riches'), written by Michael Drayton.

Here the geography of England is celebrated in a seemingly interminable narrative poem, fifteen thousand lines of tortuous syntax and classical allusion. Every now and then bits of Camden show through the verbiage, as in the description of Portland seaweed included below. Camden had written, 'amongst the sea weeds they often meet with Isidis Plocamen, *that is* Isis's hair, *a sort of shrub produc'd by the sea, not unlike coral; it has no leaves, and when cut it changes colour, growing black and hard, and the leaf fall breaks it.' Just the thing for Drayton to pick up on his way from Marshwood Vale to Weymouth via the slopes of Mount Parnassus.*

Through the Dorsetian fields that lie in open view,
My progresse I againe must seriouslie pursue,
From Marshwoods fruitfull Vale my journey on to make;
(As Phoebus getting up out of the Easterne lake,
Refresht with ease and sleepe, is to his labour prest;
Even so the labouring Muse, heere baited with this rest.)

Whereas the little Lim along doth easelie creepe,
And Car, that comming downe unto the troubled Deepe,
Brings on the neighbouring Bert, whose batning mell-
owed banke,
From all the British soyles, for Hempe most hugely ranke
Doth beare away the best; to Bert-port which hath gain'd
That praise from every place, and worthilie obtain'd
Our cordage from her store, and cables should be made,
Of any in that kind most fit for Marine trade:
Not sever'd from the shore, aloft where Chesill lifts
Her ridged snake-like sands, in wrecks and smouldring
drifts,
Which by the South-wind raysed, are heav'd on little hills:
Whose valleys with his flowes when foming Neptune fills,
Upon a thousand Swannes the naked Sea-Nymphes ride
Within the ouzie Pooles, replenisht every Tide:
Which running on, the Ile of Portland pointeth out;
Upon whose moisted skirt with sea-weed fring'd about,
The bastard Corall breeds, that drawne out of the brack,
A brittle stalke becomes, from greenish turn'd to black:
Which th'Ancients, for the love that they to Isis bare
(Their Goddesse most ador'd) have sacred for her haire.
Of which the Naides, and the blew Nereides make
Them Taudries for their necks: when sporting in the Lake,
They to their secrete Bowres the Sea-gods entertaine.
Where Portland from her top doth over-peere the Maine:
Her rugged front empal'd (on every part) with rocks,
Though indigent of wood, yet fraught with woolly flocks:
Most famous for her folke, excelling with the sling,
Of any other heere this Land inhabiting;
That there-with they in warre offensivelie might wound,
If yet the use of shot Invention had not found.
Where from the neighbouring hills her passage Wey doth
path:
Whose haven, not our least that watch the mid-day, hath
The glories that belong unto a complete Port;
Though Wey the least of all the Naides that resort
To the Dorsetian sands, from off the higher shore.

Portland, from Abbotsbury Hill

Salisbury Cathedral

Rather better is his evocation of Salisbury Plain. Notice how old Geoffrey of Monmouth still makes his presence felt at the end.

Away yee barb'rous Woods; How ever yee be plac't
On Mountaines, or in Dales, or happily be grac't
With floods, or marshie fels, with pasture, or with earth
By nature made to till, that by the yeerely birth
The large-bay'd Barne doth fill, yea though the fruitfulst
  ground.
For, in respect of Plaines, what pleasure can be found
In darke and sleepie shades? where mists and rotten fogs
Hang in the gloomie thicks, and make unstedfast bogs,

By dropping from the boughs, the o're-growen trees
  among,
With Caterpillers kells, and duskie cobwebs hong.

  The deadlie Screech-owle sits, in gloomie covert hid;
Whereas the smooth-brow'd Plaine, as liberallie doth bid
The Larke to leave her Bowre, and on her trembling wing
In climing up tow'rds heaven, her high-pitcht Hymnes to
  sing
Unto the springing Day; when gainst the Sunnes arise
The earlie Dawning strewes the goodly Easterne skies
With Roses every where: who scarcelie lifts his head
To view this upper world, but hee his beames doth spred

Stair Hole

Upon the goodlie Plaines; yet at his Noonesteds hight,
Doth scarcelie pierce the Brake with his farre-shooting
    sight.

The gentle Shepheards heer survay their gentler sheepe:
Amongst the bushie woods luxurious Satyrs keepe.
To these brave sports of field, who with desire is wonne,
To see his Grey-hound course, his Horse (in diet) runne,
His deepe mouth'd Hound to hunt, his long-wingd Haulk
    to flie,
To these most noble sports his mind who doth apply,
Resorts unto the Plaines. And not a foughten Field,
Where Kingdoms rights have laine upon the speare and
    shield,
But Plaines have beene the place; and all those Trophies hie
That ancient times have rear'd to noble memorie:
As, Stonendge, that to tell the British Princes slaine
By those false Saxons fraud, here ever shall remaine.

Perhaps at this point we need an antidote to Drayton's florid flights of fancy. A younger contemporary of the poet (he was twenty-three when Drayton's pen finally ran out), Thomas Fuller, was a solid churchman with the knack of precision. Here, in a nutshell, are his assessments of Dorset and Wiltshire, first published in 1661.

Dorsetshire

It hath a self-sufficiency of all commodities necessary for man's temporal well-being, and needs not be beholding to any neighbouring county, for it can – 1. Feed itself with fine wheat, fat flesh, dainty fowl, wild and tame, fresh fish from sea and rivers. To this meat it yieldeth that sauce without which all the rest is little worth: I mean salt, made here in some measure, but which hath been, and may be, in more abundance. 2. Clothe itself with its own wool, and broadcloth made thereof; and it is believed that no place in England affordeth more sheep in so small a compass as this county about Dorchester. And as they are provided for warmth in their woollen, so for cleanliness with their linen cloth, great store of good flax and hemp growing therein. 3. Build its own houses with good timber out of Blackmore Forest, and with (if not better, I am sure more) freestone out of Portland, most approaching that of Normandy (as in position) so in the purity thereof. Nor wanteth it veins of marble in the Isles of Purbeck. And to all this an excellent air, and the conveniency of a sea, to export for their profit, and import for their pleasure, as whose necessities were provided for before.

Wiltshire

A pleasant county, and of great variety. I have heard a wise man say that an ox left to himself would, of all England, choose to live in the north, a sheep in the south part hereof, and a man in the middle betwixt both, as partaking of the pleasure of the plain, and the wealth of the deep country. Nor is it unworthy observing, that of all inland shires (no ways bordered on salt water) this gathereth the most in the circumference thereof, as may appear by comparing them, being in compass one hundred and thirty-nine miles.

Fuller spent seven years, from 1634 to 1641, as incumbent of Broadwindsor in Dorset, and his first wife was a Wiltshire woman; but apart from him, and the anonymous monk of Malmesbury, our contributors up to now have had little personal connection with Wessex, so far as we know, and their impressions of the region are those of outsiders. Had we to rely solely on their reports, and those of men and women like them, in order to reconstruct the medieval history of Wessex, our perspective would be narrow indeed. But, of course, there survives locally and nationally a wealth of parchment and paper – legal documents, tax lists, minute books, law suits – which help us to put detail on to the outline. Here, for example, is part of a report on what the Dean of Salisbury found when, in 1405, he paid a visit to Netheravon and Chisenbury. It reveals what historians used to call solemnly 'a lax state of affairs'.

The rector fails to provide a set of vestments. An ordinal or missal is lacking through the rector's fault. The vicar has been there over a year and only resided for four weeks. The chaplain raped Joan Souter of Chisenbury. The chaplain married Joan, John Griffith's servant, and William Felawe of Upavon, in Chisenbury chapel without the vicar of Upavon's licence. The chaplain stabled his horse in Chisenbury chapel, tethering him to the font. The roof and timber-work of the north barn are defective. The chancel desks are weak and broken, the chancel roof is defective, and the chancel door is broken through the rector's fault. The vicar fails to provide his surplice. The nave roof and windows are defective; the churchwardens said on 21 January 1406 in the cathedral that they have been repaired. William Compton fornicates with Maud Wilkys. The vicar uses the church porch as his stable and

Enford

Gold Hill, Shaftesbury

keeps his horse in the churchyard. The parish clerk is married. . . . Ralph Hobbes fornicates with one Isabel. He refuses tithe of things which are yearly renewed. John Giles commits adultery with Alice, Thomas Giles's servant; he paid a fine of 6d on 14 April 1406 in the cathedral for both of them, and they were both dismissed. Ralph Hobbes threatens to kill the chaplain of Netheravon, who dares not administer sacraments in Chisenbury chapel. The vicar of Netheravon fails to say mass there on Sundays, Wednesdays and Fridays. . . .

Two centuries later Sir Francis Ashley, a Dorchester magistrate, kept a casebook. Of particular concern to him were the itinerant tradesmen and petty criminals who attended the annual Dorset fairs, such as that held on Woodbury Hill near Bere Regis. Every year a sorry procession of swindles and hard-luck stories came to his attention. In 1617, for example, Margaret Hill and Nicholas Mathew would have escaped detection had they not started quarrelling with each other.

Examination of Margaret Hill wife of William Hill of Aldersgate Street, London, Arras weaver. (She is accused by Edward Peters to have ben a cut purse manie yeares sithence she was apprehended at Sarum for the like where she was convicted and stayed for her pardon [marginal note].) She sayeth that she came from London to the fayer at Woodberrie Hill, there to meet with her husband whom she reporteth to have lived from her by the space of halfe a yeare now last past. And that being in the middle of the fayer she fownd the purse which was taken upon her, having nothing in it, but sayeth that she had then about her 4 nobles which she brought with her from London. And being asked why she maketh her pocket in the pryvey place where it was found, she sayeth it is to keep her belly warme, having no other pocket. And confesseth that the same day not long before she was taken, she offered to pawne her hat for 2s 0d, but sayeth the cause was for that

she was unwilling to change a peece of gold of 22s which she had about her.

Examination of Christine Tylser and Margaret Coomes of Beer Regis. They sayeth that yesterday, about 10 of the clock at night they being requested by the Constable of the Hundred of Beer Regis to search the said Margaret Hill for a purse wherwith she was suspected, they therupon making search accordinglie found the said purse in a pocket made in her cote before next her smocke in a privy place, but found no money in the purse, but in that pocket they found loose 4 nobles in silver, together with bond-points, gartering stuffe and such like things. And say that in the search the said Margaret Hill gott the purse in to her hands and held it away endeavouring to conceale it.

Examination of Jane Gould, wife of Henry Gould, and Margery Lockyer of Beer Regis. They say and first the said Jane sayeth that yesterday about one of the clock in the afternoone the said Margaret Hill being at this examinants' howse in Beer where she had lodged the night before, the said Margaret Hill desired her this examinant to send her boy to see whether she would borrowe 2s 0d upon her hat, saying that she was without money wherupon to give her satisfacon, The said Jane sent her boy to the other examinant Margery Lockyer making shew to borrow the money. And the said examinant Margery sayeth that the boy coming to her in such errand she refused to lend anie money. And these examinants both say that afterwards about 10 of the clocke at night of the same day the said Margaret Hill was apprehended by the Constable having then as these examinants have heard good store of monie fownd about her. And the said examinant Jane farther sayeth that the cause of such apprehension of the said Margaret Hill was upon words passing betweene her and a man that was a stranger being in the said Margaret Hill's companie wherin they did charge one an other with theft. And sayeth also that upon these words she, this examinant, having suspicion of the said stranger who nameth himselfe Nicholas Mathew, did watch as he went out into the backside of her howse and might perceive that he threw something from him and goeing to see what it was fownd that it was a purse with a key and two writs therein but no money in the purse.

Examination of Nicholas Mathew of Lower Clatford near Andover, shearman. He sayeth that he came to Dorchester on Saturday last being the 6th of this moneth to seeke a man that wrought with an unkle of his named William Mathew, being a shearman, and lying in Clatford aforesaid. And that retorning towards Woodberrie Hill he overtooke by the way the said Margaret Hill and came along in her companie to a parish three miles from Beer where they lay that night. And on Sunday they came along together to Beer where they lay Sunday night at the howse of Henry Gould. And confesseth that they the said Margaret and this examinant did there fall out, revyling and rayling the one at the other, with fowle language, he this examinant charging her that she was a cutpurse and wished she might be searched. And she the said Margaret on the other side telling this examinant that she would not mayntane such a rogue as he was. Upon which occasion the Constable was sent for and search made. But he denieth that he had anie purse or threw away any.

And what should we make of Alice Balston in 1620? Was she thief or prostitute, or both, or neither?

Examination of Alice Balston, singlewoman. Stated that she was in Thomas Sowthyes booth on Woodbury Hill at the last fair, and had taken too much to drink. One Gillett attempted her chastity and sollicited her to have his pleasure of her, which she refusing to grant him the said Gillett brake off his purse from the place where it was tyed and delivered the same unto her, saying that if she would consent to ly with him he would give it her. Which cawsed her at last to yeld unto him. And the said Gillett having had his desyres did then requier his purse againe, which she refused to deliver. Afterwards one Ash who lay in the

same room persuaded her to lie with him by giving her an handkerchief in which was 7s 0d. Later she put the money from both men in her shoe fearing that they would take it from her. At the time there were three other people in the room, but they were all asleep being about xii a clock at night.

Examination of Thomas Gillett of Dorchester, shoo-maker. Stated that he had lodged at Woodbury Hill in Thomas Sowthye's bower, upon hydes of tanned leather that were in the Bower, and there slept till day, and in the morning his purse was gone and the strings had been cut, he suspected Alice Balston who had slept in the same room. He charged her with the theft and she was searched by some of the women who were present, who found 13s 3d in her shoe. He denied that he had anie carnall knowledge with her or that he ever attempted it.

Examination of Richard Ash of Fordington, shoo-maker. Agreed with Thomas Gillett and had also lost his money. He suspected Alice Balston and likewise denied any sexual intercourse.

The squalor, violence and uncertainty of life among the poor in an unhealthy city usually escaped the notice of educated and aristocratic visitors in the seventeenth century – the kind of people who wrote down their impressions. Not that Salisbury would have attracted many visitors in 1627, one of several years in which it suffered a devastating epidemic of plague. On the contrary, everyone who had anywhere else to go packed their bags and left. But John Ivie, the city's mayor, remained at his post, and more than thirty years later wrote an account of his attempts to keep order amid the crumbling fabric of a disease-ridden and terrified populace. Here is a taste of his unsavoury story.

It pleased God for the first part of the year all things went well until after Christmas was spent. But after Candlemas was past the Lord sent upon us a very sore and grievous plague. And as many persons of the city that had any friends in the country that would receive them into

Corsley

Mere, from Castle Hill

part of their houses or barns did fly as if it were out of an house on fire; insomuch they did load forth of goods and wares above three score carts a day until all of any ability were gone, and this in four days.

And then there was none left to assist me and comfort the poor in so great a misery, neither recorder, justice, churchwarden, or overseers in all the city, nor high constable, but only two of the petty constables that had no friend to receive them in the country. Wherefore I got them to stay with me and they did prove to me a great comfort both by night and by day; and I did give them ten shillings apiece by the week. . . . They are yet both living, by name Christopher Brathat and John Pinhorne, which were to me as sent from God both night and day to carry out the infected persons to the pesthouses and to help order the unruly bearers and a multitude of rude people,

which was like both night and day to ruinate the whole city. But God being merciful unto us did put into my heart to rule so great a multitude. I had sent away my wife and maid; I had then my chief sergeant in my house and one man and an old servant maid that had been with me many years. We did all make a vow and promise together that whosoever it pleased God to visit of us the others should be faithful to him. . . .

The first which was called to watch was one William Painter, a hellier [tiler], who answered, 'I will not watch unless I have pay.' . . . I leaped off the bench and seized on him, requiring help, and dragged him to the gaol stairs where he took hold of one of the posts and did roar and beg for pardon and would watch. But I refused to accept him a while until all the rest said, 'We will all watch.' Then I called him again and he was sworn and did watch. . . .

And so by God's mercy we had a good watch all the year after.

Besides this I had a sad hand with the bearers for I could get at first but three and two to carry the first corpse to the grave, who was Giles Capon. They would have of me four shillings apiece; then they bore the corpse to the grave. And to house them was much to do. In the churchyard were two tenements which I put both into one house. The two tenants were put into one part thereof and the three bearers were put into the other. As soon as I was come home, one of the neighbours told me that Mr. Robert Belman had pulled her out of her house because she was wife to one of the bearers. Presently this Belman came to me and I asked why he had thrown that poor woman out of doors and her goods. He told me that she should not be there for her husband would come to her in the night, and so he with his wife and family should be infected with the plague. I required him to take in this poor woman and help her in with her goods again: 'If not, give me your answer.' He replied, 'I will not.' 'Then will I make you lie in the gaol.' Presently I fell upon him and took hold of him. Then he said he would give bail, but I would not take it, but said, 'As soon as you are in the gaol I will break up the door and put the poor woman into her own possession again.' By this time he was halfway to the gaol. Then came many of his friends and entreated for him. So at last the woman was in her house again. . . .

This night being past, I had peace a long time until the bearers were in rebellion. They came to the council house and would speak with me. One Mr. Windover came and told me there were four gentlemen at the stairs' foot would speak with me. I desired him to entreat them to come up; he told me they would not. I went down and there I found my four bearers, each of them with a good hedge stake in his hand. I said, 'What make you here?' They replied with oaths they would have better allowance; they would not live with four shillings a week apiece. I stepped down by them and said, 'You shall,' and looked about for stones in the street and put them into the skirt of my gown until it was full, and called to men and boys to fling stones at them as I did. They did the like. The bearers gathered stones and threw them again at me but it was God's will that I should hit one of them on the head. Then the stones came so fast upon them that they began to run. . . .

Three days after one desired me to walk to the churchyard where I should see good sport with the searching woman and the bearers. I came to a place where I could see and hear them, and when I came I found the four bearers, each of them having on their shoulders a thurndel [three-pint] pot of ale, and the woman had on her head a thurndel pot of ale. These five were dancing amongst the graves singing, 'Hie for more shoulder-work!' in a fearful manner. And when they saw me they ran away. Shortly after one of them died, which put me to much care for another, for then the plague did much increase and in that summer died nine bearers. . . .

In that time there was one Bull, a wood-cleaver, and two of his children were all three sick of the plague and speechless. I was told of it by the attender of their house. I went to the door of the house to talk with his wife. I asked her, 'How do you all? How is it with you, your husband, and your children?' She said, 'My husband and two of my children cannot speak to me, and I looks for a good hour.' 'I pray take it not amiss,' [I replied,] 'I must in the night remove you all to the pesthouse. Therefore provide what you will have carried with you.'

She railed on me very sorely. Yet late in the night I came to have them all out, but she would not open the door, but in a rude manner did scold at me, and asked me whether I came of a woman or a beast that I should do so bloody an act upon poor people in their condition. I bid the bearers break open the door but they would not or could not. Whereupon I sent my man home for my iron bar. Yet she would not open her door. I gave the bearers orders to strike in the bar between the durns [doorposts] and the door and at the second stroke the door flew open. Then

Fiddleford Mill, on the River Stour

two of them went in and came out again immediately and told me their lives were as precious to them as mine to me; they would not go in again; the house was so hot they were not able to stay there. For the smell of the house, with the heat of the infection, was so grievous they were not able to endure it. I told them, 'You must and shall endure it.' I had then with me my two petty constables, my sergeant, and my man, and from the pesthouse two able men to bear the barrow. Those two men with the four bearers did carry these three speechless people to the pesthouse, but the bearers stood to their word: they would not go in again. So we placed ourselves above and below

them, for if need were we had good weapons. But we did so beat them with stones that they were forced to go into the house for shelter. It was a close house and but one little door to the street and a little window. So they brought out the sick and whole and carried them into the fields to the pesthouse, and they were all there in two rooms. And then God so ordered for them through his mercy that they all came home again in health, to my comfort.

On a lighter note one of John Ivie's contemporaries, a certain William Whiteway, citizen of Dorchester, was making a commonplace book and diary covering precisely the period of

Salisbury's misfortunes. He too had dreadful events to chronicle, including the great Dorchester fire of January 1622, but he could also record a funnier side of life. Here are three of his anecdotes, which betray a certain ambivalence to the rule of law.

An officer of the custome at Melcombe went abord a ship to search, and perceived a good quantity of leather (a commodity upon which duty was payable) and said to the owner that stood by, 'What do I see yonder; methinks I see leather!' The merchant said nothing, but clapt two pieces of gold before his eyes and asked him what he did see now? The officer said, 'Nothing,' and sware that gold was the worst metall in the worlde to make spectacles.

Mr. Hobson, Town Clerk of Dorchester, one day going to Waymouth to plead in their Court with his black box of writings some good fellowes got him into an alehouse by the way, and while he was drinking took out his papers and filled his box full of bees that had newly swarmed. When he came to the Court and opened his box the bees flew out with such a hum that the Maior and all the rest ran out of the hall about the streets with the bees about their ears, which peppered many of them.

Mr. Tregonwell, some time gentelman of the bedchamber to King Henry 8, when a company of Cornishmen came to the King with a petition about some abbey land, he asked what they would have, and when they refused to impart their busynes unto him he waited till the King came forth, and when they kneeled downe to put their petition he kneeled downe with them; and when they thanked the King for granting their request he also thanked the King with them and afterwards went to them and told them he did look for a share in that the King had granted them, whatever it were. They refused, whereupon he went to the King and crost all that the King had granted them. Then they came backe again to the King and told him how one of his gentelmen went about to crost that which his maiesty had so gratiously bestowed upon them. The King told them that it was very reasonable that he should have a

share with them, for it was for his sake especially that he granted their petition, thinking at that time that he had had interest in it, and with all counselled them to give him content. But Tregonwell dealt so effectually with them that he drew from them a faire estate, and from him are descended the Tregonwells of Dorsettshire.

John Aubrey, our next contributor, has acquired a reputation as a gossip, based on his portrait gallery of BRIEF LIVES, an

Broad Chalke

the chalk country of Salisbury Plain as in the 'cheese' country of north Wiltshire. A voracious collector of information and a voluminous scribbler, he was less good at organizing his work, and most of his writing remained in note form and unpublished at the time of his death in 1697, to be resurrected years – centuries even – afterwards. Among these works were the NATURAL HISTORY OF WILTSHIRE *and the* WILTSHIRE COLLECTIONS, *which are both readily accessible in Victorian editions.*

First we shall sample Aubrey the collector of good stories.

Old Symon Brunsdon of Winterborn-Basset, in Wilts: he had been parish-clarke there *tempore Mariae Reginae* [in the time of Queen Mary]: The Tutelar Saint of that Church is Saint Katharine; he lived downe till the beginning of King James the first: when the Gad-flye had happened to sting his Oxen, or Cowes, and made them run-away in that Champagne-countrey, he would run after them, crying out, 'Good St. Katherine of Winterbourne stay my Oxen: Good St. Katherine of Winterborne, stay my Oxen,' etc.: This old Brunsdon was wont in the summer-time to leave his Oxen in the field, and goe to the Church to pray to Saint Katherine: by that time he came to his Oxen perhaps the Gadfly might drive them away: upon such an occasion he would cry out to St. Katherine, as is alrady sayd. – From my old cosen Ambrose Brown of Winterbourne Basset.

Dame Olave, a daughter and coheir of Sir Henry Sharington of Lacock being in Love with John Talbot (a younger Brother of the Earle of Shrewsbury) and her Father not consenting that she should marry him: discoursing with him one night from the Battlements of the Abbey-Church; said shee, 'I will leap downe to you': her sweet Heart replied, he would catch her then; but he did not believe she would have done it: she leap't downe and the wind (which was then high) came under her coates: and did something breake the fall: Mr. Talbot caught her in his armes, but she struck him dead; she cried out for help, and he was with great difficulty brought to life again:

entertaining, and often scurrilous, collection of anecdotal biographies of his contemporaries and of earlier celebrities. But those who dismiss him as a prattling old scandalmonger do him a serious injustice. Not only did he possess an accomplished literary style, but he was also a serious and influential scholar of powerful – if slightly disorganized – intellect and, as an original Fellow of the Royal Society, possessed a distinguished circle of friends in the scientific, literary and antiquarian worlds of his day.

He was born into a landed family at Easton Piercy near Chippenham in 1625, but he also had relations and an estate at Broad Chalke in south Wiltshire, and so was equally at home in

Downs to the north of the Vale of Pewsey

Lacock

her father told her that since she had made such a leap she should e'en marrie him. She was my honoured friend Col. Sharington Talbot's Grand Mother: and died at her house at Lacock about 1651, being about an hundred years old.

Some cow-stealers will make a hole in a hott lofe newly drawn out of the oven, and putt it on an oxes horn for a convenient time, and then they can turn their softned hornes the contrary way, so that the owner cannot swear to his own beast. Not long before the King's restauration a fellow was hanged at Tyburn for this, and say'd that he had never come thither if he had not heard it spoken of in a sermon. Thought he, I will try this trick.

Part of Aubrey's appeal lies in the way in which, during a descriptive or scientific passage, he repeatedly interrupts himself to describe some personal recollection or opinion which may be only loosely connected with the matter in hand. Here we find him embarking on a description of the Wiltshire downs.

These downes runne into Hampshire, Berkshire, and Dorsetshire; but as to its extent in this county, it is from Red-hone, the hill above Urshfont, to Salisbury, north and south, and from Mere to Lurgershall, east and west. The turfe is of a short sweet grasse, good for the sheep, and delightfull to the eye, for its smoothnesse like a bowling green, and pleasant to the traveller; who wants here only variety of objects to make his journey lesse tedious: for here is *nil nisi campus et aer* [nothing but plain and sky], not a tree, or rarely a bush to shelter one from a shower.

The soile of the downes I take generally to be a white earth or mawme. More south, about Wilton and Chalke, the downes are intermixt with boscages that nothing can be more pleasant, and in the summer time doe excell Arcadia in verdant and rich turfe and moderate aire, but in winter indeed our air is cold and rawe. The innocent lives here of the shepherds doe give us a resemblance of the golden age. Jacob and Esau were shepherds; and Amos, one of the royall family, asserts the same of himself, for he was among the shepherds of Tecua following that employment. . . .

Then, after a dozen lines which include Moses, Ovid, St Basil and Lucretius, Aubrey ventures an opinion.

And, to speake from the very bottome of my heart, not to mention the integrity and innocence of shepherds, upon which so many have insisted and copiously declaimed, methinkes he is much more happy in a wood that at ease contemplates the universe as his own, and in it the sunn and starrs, the pleasing meadows, shades, groves, green banks, stately trees, flowing springs, and the wanton windings of a river, fit objects for quiet innocence, than he that with fire and sword disturbs the world, and measures his possessions by the wast that lies about him.

These plaines doe abound with hares, fallow deer, partridges, and bustards. In this tract is the Earl of Pembroke's noble seat at Wilton; but the Arcadia and Daphne is about Vernditch and Wilton; and these romancy plaines and boscages did no doubt conduce to the hightening of Sir Philip Sydney's phansie. He lived much in these parts, and his most masterly touches of his pastoralls he wrote here upon the spott, where they were conceived. 'Twas about these purlieus that the muses were wont to appeare to Sir Philip Sydney, and where he wrote down their dictates in his table book, though on horseback. For those nimble fugitives, except they be presently registred, fly away, and perhaps can never be caught again. But they were never so kind to appeare to me, though I am the usufructuary [tenant: a reference to Aubrey's farm at Broad Chalke]: it seems they reserve that grace only for the proprietors, to whom they have continued a constant kindnesse for a succession of generations of the no lesse ingenious than honorable family of the Herberts [Earls of Pembroke]. These were the places where our Kings and Queens used to divert themselves in the hunting season. Cranbourn Chase, which reaches from Harnham Bridge, at Salisbury, near to Blandford, was belonging to Roger Mortimer, Earle of March: his seate was at his castle at Cranbourne. If these oakes here were vocall as Dodona's, some of the old dotards (old stagge-headed oakes, so called) could give us an account of the amours and secret whispers between this great Earle and the faire Queen Isabell.

To find the proportion of the downes of this countery to the vales, I did divide Speed's Mappe of Wiltshire with a paire of cizars, according to the respective hundreds of downes and vale, and I weighed them in a curious ballance of a goldsmith, and the proportion of the hill countery to the vale is as —— [left blank] to —— [left blank], sc. about three-quarters almost.

There we glimpse the true Aubrey. He devised a clever experiment ('ingeniose' would have been his word), but then he mislaid the result.

Avebury

For our final dive into Aubrey's notes, we shall pick out part of his description of what was to be his most important contribution to the study of archaeology, then in its infancy, his 'discovery' of the stone circles at Avebury.

I was inclined by my Genius from my childhood, to the love of antiquities: and my Fate dropt me in a countrey most suitable for such enquiries. Salisbury-plaines and Stonehenge I had known from eight years old: but I never saw the Countrey about Marleborough till Christmas 1648: being then invited to the Lord Francis Seymour's, by the Honorable Mr. Charles Seymour, then of Allington near Chippenham. . . .

The morrow after Twelfday, Mr. Charles Seymour and Sir William Button of Tokenham, Baronet, mett with their packs of hounds at the Grey-Wethers. These Downes look as if they were sowen with great Stones, very thick; and in a dusky evening they looke like a flock of Sheep: from whence it takes its name: one might fancy it to have been the scene where the giants fought with huge stones

Corsham

Off for a jaunt

against the Gods. 'Twas here that our game began, and the chase lead us, at length, thorough the village of Aubury, into the closes there: where I was wonderfully surprized at the sight of those vast stones, of which I had never heard before: as also at the mighty Bank and graffe [ditch] about it. I observed in the inclosure some segments of rude circles, made with these stones, whence I concluded, they had been in the old time complete. I left my company a while, entertaining myselfe with a more delightfull indagation: and then steered by the cry of the Hounds, overtooke the company, and went with them to Kynnet, where was a good hunting-dinner provided. Our repast was cheerfull, which being ended, we remounted and beat over the downs with our grey-hounds. In this afternoon's diversion I happened to see Wensditch [Wansdyke], and an old camp, and two or three sepulchres. The evening put a period to our sport, and we returned to the Castle at Marleborough, where we were nobly entertained. . . . I think I am now the only surviving gentleman of that company.

In the year 1655 was published by Mr. Web, a book intituled 'Stonehenge Restored', but writt by Mr. Inigo Jones; which I read with great delight. There is a great deale of learning in it, but having compared his scheme with the monument itself, I found he had not dealt fairly, but had made a *Lesbian's rule*, which is conformed to the stone; that is, he framed the monument to his own hypothesis, which is much differing from the thing itself. This gave me an edge to make more researches; and a farther opportunity was, that my honored and faithfull

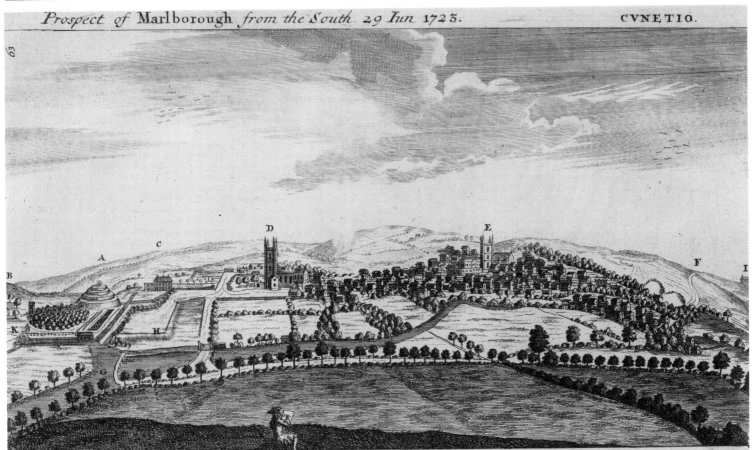

Prospect of Marlborough *from the South* 29 *Jun* 1723.   CVNETIO.

A. *Marlborough Mount.* B. *the Road to Kennet.* C. *the Castle.* D. *S.t Peters Church.* E. *S.t Marys.* F. *the Road to Ramsbury.* G. *the Kennet.* H. *the remains of the Roman Castrum.* I. *Lady Winchilseas.* K. *Preshute.*

friend Colonell James Long, of Draycot, since Baronet, was wont to spend a week or two every autumne at Aubury in hawking, where several times I have had the happiness to accompany him. Our sport was very good, and in a romantick countrey, sc.; the prospects noble and vast, the downs stock't with numerous flocks of sheep, the turfe rich and fragrant with thyme and burnet. . . . Nor are the nut-brown shepherdesses without their graces. . . .

1663. King Charles IId. discoursing one morning with my Lord Brounker and Dr. Charleton concerning Stoneheng, they told his Majestie, what they had heard me say concerning Aubury, sc. that it did as much excell Stoneheng as a Cathedral does a Parish Church. His Ma'tie admired that none of our Chorographers had taken notice of it: and commanded Dr. Charlton to bring me to him the next morning. I brought with me a draught of it donne by memorie only: but well enough resembling it, with which his Ma'tie was pleased: gave me his hand to kisse, and

Amesbury

Devizes Market-Place

commanded me to waite on him at Marleborough when he went to Bath with the Queen about a fortnight after, which I did: and the next day, when the Court were on their journey, his Ma'tie left the Queen and diverted to Aubury, where I shewed him that stupendious Antiquity, with the view whereof He and his Royal Highness the Duke of Yorke were very well pleased. His Ma'tie then commanded me to write a Description of it, and present it to him: and the Duke of Yorke commanded me to give an account of the old Camps and Barrows on the Plaines.

As his Ma'tie departed from Aubury to overtake the Queen he cast his eie on Silbury-hill about a mile off: which he had the curiosity to see, and walkt up to the top of it, with the Duke of Yorke; Dr. Charleton and I

attending them. They went to Lacock to dinner: and that evening to Bathe; all the Gentry and Commonaltie of those parts waiting on them, with great acclamations of joy, etc.

With Charles II shinning up Silbury Hill we are firmly back in the world of the tourist, and it is time to return to the literature of travel. Celia Fiennes and Daniel Defoe, the most celebrated travellers around England of the generation after Aubrey, were almost exactly contemporary with each other, and would have been toddlers when the king visited Avebury. Celia Fiennes was born and lived in Wiltshire, at Newton Tony near Salisbury, and it was from here before 1682, probably while still in her teens, that she set out on the first of her famous journeys. Her excursion, in which she may have been accompanied by her mother, took her through Dorset, from Poole to Lyme. Her account of it was not published until more than two hundred years later.

From thence [Poole] by boate we went to a little Isle called Brownsea 3 or 4 leagues off, where there is much Copperice made, the stones being found about the Isle in

Lyme Regis

Whitchurch Canonicorum

the shore in great quantetyes, there is only one house there which is the Governours, besides little fishermens houses, they being all taken up about the Copperice workes; they gather the stones and place them on the ground raised like the beds in gardens, rows one above the other, and are all shelving so that the raine disolves the stones and it draines down into trenches and pipes made to receive and convey it to the house; that is fitted with iron panns foursquare and of a pretty depth at least 12 yards over, they place iron spikes in the panns full of branches and so as the liquor boyles to a candy it hangs on those branches: I saw some taken up it look't like a vast bunch of grapes, the coullour of the Copperace not being much differing, it lookes cleare like suger-candy, so when the water is boyled to a candy they take it out and replenish the panns with more liquor; I do not remember they added anything to it only the stones of Copperice disolved by the raine into liquor as I mention'd at first; there are great furnaces under, that keepes all the panns boyling; it was a large room or building with

severall of these large panns; they do add old iron and nailes to the Copperass Stones. This is a noted place for lobsters and crabs and shrimps, there I eate some very good.

From Merly we went to the Isle of Purbeck. At Warrum we passed over a bridge where the sea flowed in and came by the ruines of Corffe Castle, which stands on a hill yet surrounded by much higher hills that might easily command it, and so in the Civill warrs was batter'd down with Grenadeers, thence you rise a great ascent of hills called the Linch, or rather the ridge, being so for 3 or 4 miles, rideing to Quare which was 16 miles from Merly to a relations house Cos'n Colliers.

From this ridge you see all the Island over, which lookes very fruitfull, good lands meadows woods and inclosures; there are many quarys in these hills of that which is called the free stone, from hence they digg it. The shores are very rocky all about the Island, we went 3 miles off to Sonidge a sea faire place not very big; there is a flatt sand by the sea

Poole Harbour

a little way; they take up stones by the shores that are so oyly as the poor burn it for fire, and its so light a fire it serves for candle too, but it has a strong offensive smell. At a place 4 miles off called Sea Cume the rockes are so craggy and the creekes of land so many that the sea is very turbulent, there I pick'd shells and it being a spring-tide I saw the sea beat upon the rockes at least 20 yards with such a foame or froth, and at another place the rockes had so large a cavity and hollow that when the sea flowed in it runne almost round, and sounded like some hall or high arch. In this Island are severall pretty good houses though not very large, att Kingston Sir William Muex has a pretty house, and att Income Mr. Collifords, Doonshay Mr. Dollings, and 7 mile off Quare att Tinnum Lady Larences there is a pretty large house but very old timber built, there I eate the best lobsters and crabs being boyled in the sea water and scarce cold, very large and sweet; most of the houses in the Island are built of stone there is so many Quarryes of stone, this is just by the great cliffs which are a vast height from the sea; here is plenty of provision of all sorts especially of fish. From Tinnum we ascend a high hill of a great length till you are out of the Island, which does hardly appeare to be now an Isle, the tide haveing left it on this side that you passe only a little brooke – there is another Castle called Bindon, but that lyes low and appears not much – thence we came to Piddle 6 or 7 miles off where was a relation Mr. Oxenbridge [who lives in] an old house which formerly was an abby; thence to Dorchester town 5 mile, it stands on the side of a hill, the river runns below it, the town lookes compact and the street's are very neatly pitch'd and of a good breadth, the Market-place is spaceious, the Church very handsome and full of galleryes.

Thence we went to Burport – about 8 miles, the wayes are stony and very narrow, the town has a steep hill to descend through the whole place; thence to Woolfe 4 miles to a relations Mr. Newbery, a man of many whymseys [who] would keep no women servants, had all washing ironing dairy, etc., all performed by men, his house look's like a little village when you come into the yard, so many little buildings apart from each other, one for a stillitory another for out-houses and offices another long building for silk wormes, and the dwelling house is but mean and spoyl'd by his fancy of makeing a hall up 3 storyes high, so lofty nothing suiteable to it; he had good gardens and orchards, much good fruite but all in a most rude confused manner. Thence we went to Colway near Lime. . . . about 8 miles to a relations house Mr. Hendlys, from thence it is 2 miles to Lime, a seaport place open to the main ocean, and so high a bleake sea that to secure the Harbour for shipps they have been at a great charge to build a Mold from the town with stone, like a halfe moon, which they call the Cobb, its raised with a high wall and this runns into the sea a good compass, that the Shipps ride safely within it; when the tide is out we may see the foundations of some part of it; that is the tyme they looke over it to see any breach and repaire it immediately, else the tide comes with so much violence would soon beate it down; there is some part of it low and only is to joyne the rest to the land, and at high water is all cover'd of such a depth of water that shipps may pass over it to enter the Cobb or Halfe Moone, which is difficult for foreigners to attempt, being ignorant, though its better than goeing round the other way, for those that know and do observe the tide; the Spring tides and on any storme does some-tymes beate up and wash over the walls of the forte or castle into the court, and so runns into the town, though at other tymes when its the ordinary tide and calme sea, it is at least 300 yards from the banke on which the high wall is built. . . .

From Lime the wayes are also difficult by reason of the very steep hills up and down, and that so successively as little or no plaine even ground, and full of large smooth pebbles that make the strange horses slip and uneasye to go; the horses of the country are accustomed to it and travell well in the rodes; in the opener wayes they use a

Milton Abbas

Stourhead

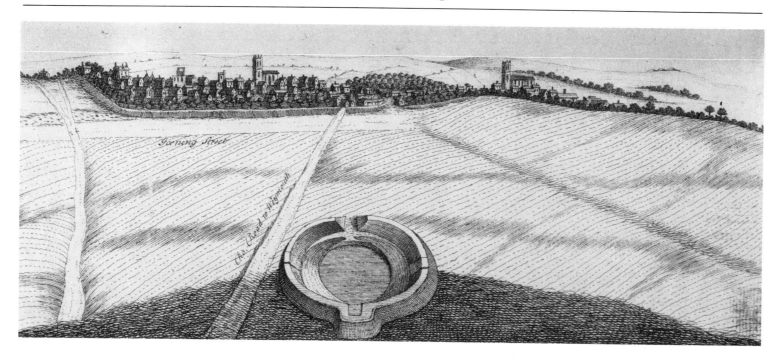

sort of waine or carriage made narrower than our southern waggon but longer, and so load them high.

Daniel Defoe was a man of many parts, and his varied career, which included business, bankruptcy, work as a political agent and spells in gaol, was matched by a prolific literary output, on subjects as diverse as religious nonconformity, English tradesmen, and the plague year. His TOUR THROUGH THE WHOLE ISLAND OF GREAT BRITAIN was published in parts between 1724 and 1726, and like his best-known works, the novels ROBINSON CRUSOE and MOLL FLANDERS, it is a product of his old age, shot through with mature reflection on the state of human affairs. Here are three passages which illustrate this worldly-wise traveller's thoughts on Wessex and its people. First, Dorchester society and the sheep-farming economy.

From hence we turn'd up to Dorchester, the county town, tho' not the largest town in the county; Dorchester is indeed a pleasant agreeable town to live in, and where I thought the people seem'd less divided into factions and parties, than in other places; for though here are divisions and the people are not all of one mind, either as to religion, or politicks, yet they did not seem to separate with so much animosity as in other places: Here I saw the Church of England clergymen, and the Dissenting minister, or preacher, drinking tea together, and conversing with civility and good neighbourhood, like catholick Christians, and men of a catholick, and extensive charity: The town is populous, tho' not large, the streets broad, but the buildings old, and low; however, there is good company and a good deal of it; and a man that coveted a retreat in this world might as agreeably spend his time, and as well in Dorchester, as in any town I know in England.

The downs round this town are exceeding pleasant, and come up on every side, even to the very streets end; and

Water-mill near Lyme Regis

West Bay, Bridport

here it was that they told me, that there were 600 thousand sheep fed on the downs, within six miles of the town; that is, six miles every way, which is twelve miles in diameter, and thirty six miles in circumference. This I say, I was told, I do not affirm it to be true; but when I viewed the country round, I confess I could not but incline to believe it.

It is observable of these sheep, that they are exceeding fruitful, and the ews generally bringing two lambs, and they are for that reason bought by all the farmers thro' the east part of England, who come to Burford Fair in this country to buy them, and carry them into Kent and Surry eastward, and into Buckinghamshire, and Bedfordshire, and Oxfordshire north, even our Bansted Downs in Surrey, so fam'd for good mutton, is supply'd from this place: The grass, or herbage of these downs is full of the sweetest, and the most aromatick plants, such as nourish the sheep to a strange degree, and the sheeps dung again nourishes that herbage to a strange degree; so that the valleys are render'd extreamly fruitful, by the washing of the water in hasty showers from off these hills.

An eminent instance of this is seen at Amesbury in Wiltshire, the next county to this, for it is the same thing in proportion over this whole county: I was told that at this town there was a meadow on the bank of the river Avon, which runs thence to Salisbury, which was let for £12 a year per acre for the grass only: This I enquir'd particularly after, at the place, and was assur'd by the inhabitants as one man, that the fact was true, and was shew'd the meadows; the grass which grew on them was such as grew to the length of ten or twelve foot, rising up to a good height, and then taking root again, and was of so rich a nature as to answer very well such an extravagant rent.

The reason they gave for this, was the extraordinary richness of the soil, made so, as above, by the falling, or washing of the rain from the hills adjacent, by which tho' no other land thereabouts had such a kind of grass, yet all other meadows, and low grounds of the valley were extremely rich in proportion.

Next, the conduct of the ladies of Lyme Regis, a theme to which we shall return later.

While we stay'd here some time viewing this town and coast, we had opportunity to observe the pleasant way of conversation, as it is manag'd among the gentlemen of this county, and their families, which are without reflection some of the most polite and well bred people in the isle of Britain: As their hospitality is very great, and their bounty to the poor remarkable, so their generous friendly way of living with, visiting, and associating one with another is as hard to be describ'd, as it is really to be admir'd; they seem to have a mutual confidence in, and friendship with one another, as if they were all relations; nor did I observe the sharping tricking temper, which is too much crept in among the gameing and horse-racing gentry in some parts of England, to be so much known among them, any otherwise than to be abhorr'd; and yet they sometimes play too, and make matches, and horse-races, as they see occasion.

The ladies here do not want the help of assemblies to assist in match-making; or half-pay officers to run away with their daughters, which the meetings, call'd assemblies in some other parts of England, are recommended for: Here's no Bury Fair, where the women are scandalously said to carry themselves to market, and where every night they meet at the play, or at the assembly for intreague, and yet I observ'd that the women do not seem to stick on hand so much in this country, as in those countries, where those assemblies are so lately set up; the reason of which I cannot help saying, if my opinion may bear any weight, is, that the Dorsetshire ladies are equal in beauty, and may be superiour in reputation; In a word, their reputation seems here to be better kept; guarded by better conduct, and manag'd with more prudence, and yet

HENRY AKERMAN
LICENSED RETAILER OF
BEER, FOREIGN & BRITISH
WINES AND SPIRITS.
DEALER IN TOBACCO.
GOOD STABLING.

Shrewton

Aldbourne

the Dorsetshire ladies, I assure you, are not nuns, they do not go vail'd about streets, or hide themselves when visited; but a general freedom of conversation, agreeable, mannerly, kind, and good runs thro' the whole body of the gentry of both sexes, mix'd with the best of behaviour, and yet govern'd by prudence and modesty; such as I no where see better in all my observation, thro' the whole isle of Britain.

And finally, London's debt to north Wiltshire.

All the lower part of this county, and also of Gloucestershire, adjoining, is full of large feeding farms, which we call dairies, and the cheese they make, as it is excellent good of its kind, so being a different kind from the Cheshire, being soft and thin, is eaten newer than that from Cheshire. Of this, a vast quantity is every week sent up to London, where, though it is called Gloucestershire cheese, yet a great part of it is made in Wiltshire, and the greatest part of that which comes to London, the Gloucestershire cheese being more generally carried to Bristol, and Bath, where a very great quantity is consumed, as well by the inhabitants of two populous cities, as also for the shipping off to our West-India colonies, and other places. This Wiltshire cheese is carried to the river of Thames, which runs through part of the county, by land carriage, and so by barges to London.

Again, in the spring of the year, they make a vast quantity of that we call green cheese, which is a thin, and very soft cheese, resembling cream cheeses, only thicker, and very rich. These are brought to market new, and eaten so, and the quantity is so great, and this sort of cheese is so universally liked and accepted in London, that all the low, rich lands of this county, are little enough to supply the market; but then this holds only for the two first summer months of the year, May and June, or little more.

Besides this, the farmers in Wiltshire, and the part of Gloucestershire adjoining, send a very great quantity of bacon up to London, which is esteemed as the best bacon in England, Hampshire only excepted: This bacon is raised in such quantities here, by reason of the great dairies, as above, the hogs being fed with the vast quantity of whey, and skim'd milk, which so many farmers have to spare, and which must, otherwise, be thrown away.

But this is not all, for as the north part of Wiltshire, as well the downs, as the vales, border upon the river Thames, and, in some places, comes up even to the banks of it; so most of that part of the county being arable land, they sow a very great quantity of barley, which is carried to the markets at Abingdon, at Farrington, and such places, where it is made into malt, and carried to London. This imploys all the hill country from above Malmsbury to Marlbro, and on the side of the Vale of White Horse, as 'tis called, which is in Barkshire, and the hills adjoining, a tract of ground, able to furnish, considering its fertility, a prodigious quantity of barley, and does so.

Thus Wiltshire itself helps to supply London with cheese, bacon, and malt, three very considerable articles, besides that vast manufacture of fine Spanish cloths, which I have said so much of, and I may, without being partial, say, that it is thereby rendered one of the most important counties in England, that is to say, important to the publick wealth of the kingdom. The bare product is in itself prodigious great; the downs are an inexhausted store-house of wooll, and of corn, and the valley, or low part of it, is the like for cheese and bacon.

Not all travellers were so well-informed and discriminating. Here is George Lipscomb, on his way back from Cornwall at the end of the eighteenth century, having the Dorset wool pulled over his eyes.

In journeying toward Salisbury, we observed upon the Downs, on the right, several barrows of different sizes, chiefly circular: – one, very large Tumulus, on the left, oval or navicularly shaped; such as Doctor Stukeley speaks

Chesil

of. In another part of the Road, we saw many small and low barrows, enclosed by a circular mound of earth.

The Counties of Dorset and Wilts are divided by a great Vallum or Ravine, called Woden's Dyke, and now, by corruption, Bogleigh or Bogley Ditch – the course of which crossing our road, we could trace it for, at least, two miles. I enquired of some Shepherds, who were tending their flocks on the Downs, where this Bank terminated – one of them said, 'a terrible ways off'. Upon asking how far that might be, we were answered, 'they zays it goes into Vrance, but I never zeed it myself.'

A few years earlier men like Lipscomb, who was twenty-six when that anecdote was published, and who later wrote a massive history of Buckinghamshire, would probably have been sent on the Grand Tour, to fill their diaries with remarkable sights and exotic adventures in Italy and the Mediterranean. But the Napoleonic Wars put a stop to such pleasures, and the English dilettante now had to content himself with exploring his own country. So we find a generation of clever and articulate young men writing about their travels in England. William Maton, for example, a Wiltshireman who explored the western counties in 1794 and 1796, was particularly interested in botany, geology and antiquities. Like Lipscomb, he was in his early twenties at the time, and went on to a distinguished medical career which included his appointment as physician to Princess (later to become Queen) Victoria. Here are two extracts from his OBSERVA-TIONS, which describe Shaftesbury, Cerne Abbas and Blackmoor Vale.

Shaftesbury barely stands within the county of Dorset, and is on the edge of a noble eminence that seems to form a natural barrier to Wiltshire, and commands a view of astonishing extent to the south-west. It is a town of great antiquity, but its present appearance ill corresponds with the account given of it by the old writers, in whose time there were twelve churches (besides the famous Bene-dictine monastery founded by Alfred,) and three mints. No part of the monastery remains, nor are there more than three churches standing, exclusive of St. James's, at the foot of the hill, which belongs to the liberty of Alcester. The houses are built with stone, but the streets have rather a mean appearance. – Few places have been distressed for water more than Shaftesbury, the situation being so high that it was necessary for the engines, erected some years ago for furnishing a supply, to raise it three hundred feet perpendicularly. These works are now neglected, a circumstance of some advantage to the poor, many of whom gain a livelihood by fetching water from a distance on their heads, or on horses' backs. – On a spot called Castle-green, at the western extremity of the town, are traces of entrenchments, and here perhaps a castle once stood, which from the nature of the situation must have been impregnable. A vast landscape appears hence, and, when illumined by the splendid rays of a morning sun, forms a scene truly glorious; though, for my own part, I was most interested in the suffusion of this astonishing expanse with the various sombre hues of evening. It is by no means destitute of feature. In front, an eminence called Duncliffe-hill rises with a beautifully wooded summit, bounding the fertile vale of Blackmoor, through which a white road sometimes losing itself among woodlands, and sometimes traversing verdant pastures, winds westward into the distance. On the left, a fine undulating ridge shelters the vale; whilst the hills of Mere in Wiltshire, and Alfred's tower at the extremity, the torr of Glastonbury, and the hazy heights of Quantock, in Somersetshire, range themselves in the remaining part of the horizon. . . .

Wishing to ascertain as accurately as possible the course of the chalk in this county, and the appearance of its boundaries, we now made a journey southward, and trod the rich soil of the vale of Blackmoor until we came to Revel-hill. The face of the country here altered, and the most pleasing intermixture of wood and pasture was exchanged for open downs and unvaried barrenness. . . . Revel-hill forms a part of the ridge (which I should distinguish by the name of the chalk boundary) coming from near Melbury somewhat in the shape of an amphi-theatre, and passing hence, with many undulations, not far south of Evershot and Beminster towards Axminster in Devonshire. The vale of Blackmoor (to which it is a boundary southward) now appears to be of a sort of elliptical shape, the longest diameter seeming to run from Melbury towards Long Burton. To the west of the latter lies the forest of Whitehart, and the country is finely wooded, presenting most rich and delightful scenery. Projecting parts of the ridge are profusely clothed on their declivities, and become noble features in the landscape, which is of a nature that rarely occurs within the confines of this county, and may justly be considered as the most beautiful that it affords.

Blackmoor Vale

We found we were now but a few miles distant from Cerne-Abbas, and, being desirous of viewing the remains of its abbey, resolved to extend our ride to it. – On our left the country began to acquire a boldness and roundness of feature that prepared us for something romantic in the situation of Cerne. – We descended into this town from an immense chalk hill terminating towards it in a mountainous prominence crowned with a very large oblong entrenchment. On the declivity of the hill (generally known by the name of Trendle-hill) may be traced a gigantic figure, cut in the chalk, in the manner of the horse on Whitehorse-hill, in Berkshire, and probably of as great antiquity. It represents a man, holding a club in his right hand, and extending the other, and appears to be almost two hundred feet in height. There is a tradition among the vulgar that this was to commemorate the destruction of a giant, who, having feasted on some sheep in Blackmoor, and laid himself down to sleep after his meal on this hill, was bound and killed by the enraged peasants on the spot. – Without resorting to any ridiculous story, or to any conceit of antiquarians, for the origin of the figure, one may conclude that most works of this sort, especially when contiguous to encampments, were the amusement merely of idle people, and cut out with as little meaning, perhaps, as shepherds' boys strip off the turf on the Wiltshire plains.

William Gilpin, a much older man, whose OBSERVATIONS ON THE WESTERN PARTS OF ENGLAND was published a year later than Maton's book, in 1798, displays similar tastes. Here is his description of the great bustard, a turkey-like bird which once inhabited Salisbury Plain.

Though Salisbury Plain in Druid times was probably a very busy scene, we now find it wholly uninhabited. Here and there we meet a flock of sheep, scattered over the side of some rising ground; and a shepherd with his dog, attending them; or perhaps we may descry some solitary waggon winding round a distant hill. But the only resident inhabitant of this vast waste is the bustard. This bird, which is the largest fowl we have in England, is fond of all extensive plains, and is found on several; but these are supposed to be his principal haunt. Here he breeds, and here he spends his summer-day, feeding with his mate on juicy berries, and the large dew-worms of the heath. As winter approaches, he forms into society. Fifty or sixty have been sometimes seen together.

As the bustard leads his life in these unfrequented wilds, and studiously avoids the haunts of men, the appearance of any thing in motion, though at a considerable distance, alarms him. I know not that he is protected, like the partridge and pheasant, by any law; but his own vigilance is a better security to him than an act of parliament. As he is so noble a prize, his flesh so delicate, and the quantity of it so large, he is of course frequently the object of the fowler's stratagems. But his caution is generally a protection against them all. The scene he frequents, affords neither tree to shelter, nor hedge to skreen, an enemy; and he is so tall, that when he raises his neck to take a perspective view, his eye circumscribes a very wide horizon. All open attempts therefore against him are fruitless. The fowler's most promising stratagem is to conceal himself in a waggon. The west country waggons, periodically travelling these regions, are objects to which the bustard is most accustomed; and though he retires at their approach, he retires with less evident signs of alarm, than from any thing else. It is possible therefore, if the fowler lie close in such a concealment, and with a long barrelled gun can direct a good aim, he may make a lucky shot. Sometimes also he slips from the tail of a waggon a couple of swift greyhounds. They soon come up with the bustard, though he runs well; and if they can contrive to reach him, just as he is on the point of taking wing (an operation which he performs with less expedition than is requisite in such critical circumstances,) they may perhaps seize him.

Gilpin's observations, according to the title of his book, were 'relative chiefly to picturesque beauty', and the aesthetic tastes of the landscape artist are uppermost in the following passage.

From Bridport to Dorchester we passed through a more inland country, though in other respects similar to the country we had just left. The features of it are broad and determined. Sweeping hills with harsh edges intersect each other. Here and there a bottom is cultivated, inclosed, and adorned with a farmhouse and a few trees; but, in general, the whole country is an extended down. It is every where fed with little rough sheep; which have formed it, with constant grazing, into the finest pasturage. Indeed a chalky soil itself, which is the substratum of these downs, is naturally inclined to produce a neat smooth surface. The several flocks which pasture these wide domains, have their respective walks; and are generally found within the distance of a mile from each other. We saw them once or twice issuing from their pens, to take their morning's repast after a hungry night. It was a pleasing sight to see such numbers of innocent animals made happy, and in the following lines it is beautifully described:

> The fold
> Poured out its fleecy tenants o'er the glebe.
> At first, progressive as a stream, they fought
> The middle field; but scattered by degrees
> In various groups, they whitened all the land.

But the progressive motion here described, is one of those incidents, which is a better subject for poetry than painting. For, in the first place, a feeding flock is seldom well grouped; they commonly separate; or, as the poet well expresses it, 'they are scattered by degrees, and whiten all the land'. Nor are their attitudes varied, as they all usually move the same way, 'progressive like a stream'. Indeed the shape of a feeding sheep is not the most pleasing, as its back and neck make a round heavy line, which in contrast only has its effect. To see a flock of sheep in their most picturesque form, we should see them reposing after their meal is over; and if they are in sunshine, they are still the more beautiful. In reposing they are generally better grouped, and their forms are more varied. Some are commonly standing, and others lying on the ground, with their little ruminating heads in various forms. And if the light be strong, it spreads over the whole one general mass; and is contrasted, at the same time, by a shadow equally strong, which the flock throws upon the ground. It may be observed also, that the fleece itself is well disposed to receive a beautiful effect of light. It does not indeed, like the smooth covering of hair, allow the eye to trace the muscular form of the animal. But it has a beauty of a different kind: the flakiness of the wool catches the light, and breaking it into many parts, yet without destroying the mass, gives it a peculiar richness.

We saw another circumstance also, in which sheep appear to advantage. The weather was sultry, the day calm, and the roads dusty. Along these roads we saw, once or twice, a flock of sheep driven, which raised a considerable cloud. As we were a little higher on the downs, and not annoyed by the dust, the circumstance was amusing. The beauty of the incident lay in the contrast between such sheep as were seen perfectly, and such as were involved in obscurity. At the same time the dust became a kind of harmonizing medium, which united the flock into one whole. It had the same effect on a group of animals, which a heavy mist, when partial, has on landscape. But though circumstances of this kind are pleasing in nature, we do not wish to see them imitated on canvas.

Yes, sheep in the Dorset countryside make a pretty picture, especially if you are a tourist. But if you live in a tumbledown cottage, and it is your job to go up on the hills in all weathers (for a pittance) to look after them, your outlook may be rather different. It is time to leave for a while our eloquent visitors, and return to the vagaries and realities of making a living. We have sampled the harshness of life in a plague-ridden city; now we must experience one of the other great hazards of urban life. We are in Blandford Forum on 4 June 1731, and the story is taken up by an inhabitant, Malachi Blake.

About Two of the Clock in the Afternoon a dismal cry of Fire was heard in our Streets. The Inhabitants of the Place were all soon alarmed, some were called from their Business, some possibly from their Pleasures, some perhaps, from their Cups. However everyone was terribly surprised, though those one would hope were in the best Posture and Temper of mind to bear it, who were most usefully or innocently imployed.

The Fire first kindled on the Out-side of a Soap boiler's House, occasioned (as he conjectures) by sparks that fell from a chimney upon the Thatch. Some think differently, but all agree that as to Man it was entirely accidental. The House stood on rising Ground where four Streets met, not far from the Middle of the Town. Our three Engines were soon brought out and play'd, but to no Purpose, for in little more than half an Hour they either were all burnt or render'd unfit for Service.

The Wind which sat North-West quickly carried the Fire into distant Parts. Every Corner of these four streets were presently in Flames that raged onward, with and against the Wind. The Fire spread itself with that speed and fury, that every Thing was soon devoured before it. Not a Piece of Timber but what was burnt to a Coal. The Pewter in many Houses was not only melted, but reduced to Ashes by the fervent Heat. Our Silver, in a literal Sense, became Dross, and if any made fine Gold their Confidence, what a sad Proof had they before their Eyes, of their extreme Folly, and its utter insufficiency to make them happy.

Most persons (which was very observable) were at once seized with such a Panic, that they gave up the Town for lost, quickly after the Fire broke out.

Before Seven of the Clock in the evening (which was about four Hours after the Fire began), there was scarce a

Rawlsbury Camp, Bulbarrow Hill

Vale of Blackmoor from Shaftesbury

House remained, but what, at least, was so much in Flames, as to be past the reach of Men to preserve it, except some few, as in Kindness to the Owners, so in Pity to them who had none left. . . .

Some few houses were remarkably preserved at the four Quarters of the Town, which we would ascribe chiefly to a good Providence – The Lord said, it is enough and the Fire was stayed. . . .

In the Day of our great Calamity, so sudden was the Fire, so furious, that many Families had scarce Time to Save any of their Effects, few had either Time or help to save much. 'Tis true, much household Goods, as well as all Sorts of Merchandise, were in the Beginning carried to distant houses, where it was apprehended they were safe from Danger, and much was brought out into the Streets, in hopes of timely Assistance to convey it away. But, alas they were soon sadly disappointed, and forced to leave to the devouring Flames, what they had with so much Pains and Difficulty brought thither. Many are now thankful they could escape with their own Lives.

The dismal Night comes on, when many who were never inured to Hardship were obliged to lie, some in Barns and Out-houses, others under the Arches of a large Bridge, and more under hedges and in the Open Air.

The Church held out against the Fury of the Flames a long time, not having any House joining to it. At length the Steeple took Fire, and that more than once, but by the great care and Diligence of some Persons it was quenched again. However about Twelve of the clock at Night the Fire was seen afresh in the Middle of the Roof. This also might have stopped at first had they had Engines, or could they have got Ladders and Vessels to carry Water. But they were all burnt. It was towards Two of the Clock in the Morning before it broke through the Roof into a Flame. Then the Fire roared dreadfully, the Lead melted, the Stones spilt and flew, nay, so fervent and irresistible was the Heat, that the Bells themselves dissolved and ran down in Streams.

Blandford old Church

It was a Mercy, however, that this spacious Pile of Building was burnt no sooner, for several who had carried their Goods into it, and betook themselves for Shelter within its Walls, were not able for some Time, without great Hazard of their Lives, either to retreat from, or to bear the scorching Heat, from the Houses that were burning around it. Whilst others were glad to lie down behind the Tomb-Stones, which were a Shadow to them

Blandford new Church

Burnt black as an Hearth, and even roasted in the Fire.

The number of those that perished had been generally reckoned to be Sixteen, but upon the best Inquiry I could make I can't find they were more than Thirteen, not one child, but most of them aged Persons viz three men and ten Women.

The Small Pox at the same Time prevailed in the town. About sixty Families, by Computation, were then visited with that Distemper. Not one indeed of the sick perished in the Flames, but then they were many of them exposed to the greatest Hazard other ways.

The Physicians, in the mean time took best care of them they were able and through the timely and benevolent Provision of some Apothecaries in the Town (who sent immediately to Salisbury and elsewhere for such Medicines as were most needed) they were soon tolerably supply'd: and within a Day or two after the Fire, two or three neighbouring Gentlemen looked in upon us and left Forty Guineas for the relief of them and the other Sufferers.

The morning after the Fire there was a great scarcity of Provision. However, some Supplies were immediately thought of and found. There were two Ovens full of Loaves, which were set in a little before the Fire began, these, tho' baked to a Crust (for the Houses were both burned to which the Ovens belonged) were very acceptable. But before Night we had fresh supplies sent in from neighbouring Parishes. The Sabbath Day after the Fire and for some days following, Waggon Loads of Bread and Beer with some Flesh were kindly and liberally sent us from the Places about us, as from Shaftesbury, Pool, Wimborne, Dorchester, Wareham, Beer, etc.

Liberal Collections were soon made in several of the adjacent Towns, and sums of Money were sent us from Private Hands. Barracks were built for the Reception of such as lay exposed to the open Air. They were built with boards and before the Winter drew on were covered with Thatch. Those who dwelt in them run up chimnies and

from the fervent Heat on one Side, as the Church itself was on the other, until the Fire about it was so far abated as to give them Opportunity to save themselves, and to carry off the Effects they had with them.

All the following Night while the Fire was slowly abating some were employed in keeping Watch over the few houses that were spared, others in searching after their lost relations and children. Some of their Friends they found dead in the Streets, part of them consumed with the Flames, while the melancholy Remains of them were

River Cerne, with Nether Cerne behind

Watercress beds, Broad Chalke

Castle Combe

stopt the Crevices with Moss and other Things. Four hundred families were burnt out and many of them reduced to great Extremity, so that several hundred Pounds of the publick Charity were extended in their present maintenance.

The whole Loss over and above all Insurances amounted to eighty-four Thousand, three hundred and forty-eight Pounds.

Blandford's fire, terrifying and disastrous though it must have been at the time, proved no more than a setback. The elegant Georgian town which rose from the ashes is ample testimony to the prosperity enjoyed by some, at least, of the inhabitants of any eighteenth-century market centre which found itself on an important road.

More crippling than such sudden catastrophes as fire to the life of Wessex generally were the abominably low wages and dismal living conditions endured by the bulk of the labouring population through much of the eighteenth and nineteenth centuries. In the 1790s Sir Frederic Eden, a young disciple of the political economist Adam Smith, prepared a report on the state of the poor in England, based on detailed fieldwork in selected places around the country. Here is part of his report on Seend, a village between Devizes and Trowbridge, on the edge of the west Wiltshire textile district. (As a guide, 5d. is equivalent to 2p, and 1s. to 5p.)

The chapelry of Seend is annexed to the vicarage of Melksham: it is about 6 miles in circumference; and contains between 600 and 700 inhabitants, of whom several are Methodists. 63 houses pay the window-tax; 150 single, and 36 double tenements, are exempted.

There is very little arable land in the chapelry: the principal employment is the cloth manufacture. The wages of agricultural labour vary from 7s. to 9s. a week: 8s. may be reckoned the average. Some men (but very few,) in addition to their weekly pay of 8s. are allowed, by the farmer, for whom they work, butter at 6d. the lb., and cheese at 4d. the lb. In hay-harvest, men are paid 1s. 6d. the day: women 8d. a day, and beer; and at other times of the year, for work in the field, 6d. the day.

The prices of provisions are: butcher's meat, from 5d. to 7d. the lb.; cheese, from 5d. to 6d.; butter, from 10d. to 11d.; bread, 4 and a quarter lb. for 1s.; and bacon, from 11d. to 1s. the lb.. . . .

There is one ale-house in Seend; and one Friendly Society, which is not in the most flourishing condition: its rules have been confirmed by the magistrates. There is neither a house of industry, nor any regular establishment for the employment of the Poor: the most necessitous reside in houses belonging to the chapelry; some receive regular weekly pensions, and others have occasional relief. . . .

As the chapelry consists almost entirely of dairy farms, and consequently affords very little employment in husbandry, except during the hay-harvest, the labouring poor are very dependant on the neighbouring towns, where the cloth manufacture is carried on; but, unfortunately, since the introduction of machinery, which lately took place, hand-spinning has fallen into disuse, and for these two reasons; the clothier no longer depends on the Poor for the yarn which they formerly spun for him at their own homes, as he finds that 50 persons, (to speak within compass,) with the help of machines, will do as much work as 500 without them; and the Poor, from the great reduction in the price of spinning, scarcely have the heart to earn the little that is obtained by it. For what they used to receive 1s. and 1s. 2d. the pound for spinning, before the application of machinery, they now are allowed only 5d.; so that a woman, in a good state of health, and not incumbered with a family, can only earn 2s. 6d. a week, which is at the rate of one pound of spinning-work the day, and is the utmost that can be done: but if she has a family, she cannot earn more than 2d. a day, or 1s. a week; or spin more than 2 pounds and a half in a week: the consequence is, that their maintenance must chiefly

Cherhill

The River Piddle, near Throop

depend on the exertions of the man, (whose wages have not increased in proportion to this defalcation from the woman's earnings,) and, therefore, the present dear times are very severely felt by all families, and even by single women, who depend solely upon spinning for their support. Of this, the following statement of the earnings and expences of a labourer is an evincing proof:

The man earns 8s. a week; the wife and oldest child, 4s. 6d.; the parish allows 1s. 6d.; total weekly receipts, 14s.. Bread costs (for about 8 lb. a day), 11s. a week; Butter, 3 lb. bought of his master at the reduced price, 1s. 6d.; Remains for cloaths, and other necessaries, 1s. 6d..

This man lives in a house that was built on part of the waste; but the Lord of the manor not having demanded his due for many years, it may now be considered as a freehold. It is in a very ruinous condition; but the man cannot afford to repair it himself: nor does he like to apply to the parish to do it; thinking that, in that case, they would lay claim to it. The rent of cottages in this county, in general, is very high; from £1 10s. to £3, a year: most of the labouring poor, however, in this chapelry, either reside in houses belonging to the parish, or receive paro-

chial assistance to the amount of their rent, unless they are of that description of workmen, whose earnings are very considerable; as sawyers or weavers, who earn from 17s. to £1 1s. a week: but even this class of people cannot easily spare any thing for rent, if their families are large.

Nothing is stated above for fuel. If the labourer is employed in hedging and ditching, he is allowed to take home a faggot every evening, while that work lasts: but this is by no means sufficient for his consumption: his children, therefore, are sent into the fields, to collect wood where they can; and neither hedges nor trees are spared by the young marauders, who are thus, in some degree, educated in the art of thieving; till, from being accustomed to small thefts, they hesitate not to commit greater depredations on the public: this, perhaps, might be prevented, if every parish would lay in a stock of fuel, and sell it at somewhat below the market-price, instead of giving their Poor an allowance in money to purchase it. . . .

It is obvious, that employment for the Poor is much wanted: a few years ago, it was proposed to the parish-officers to solicit the farmers to advance one year's Poor's Rate, for the purchase of raw materials, to set the Poor to work; and to give them the old prices for their work: these suggestions, however, were not attended to; and the Rates continue to increase.

In some of the neighbouring corn parishes, the reduction in the price of spinning has been more severely felt than at Seend. In one instance, however, the Poor have been better off: they were allowed wheat by their employers at the reduced price of 8s. the bushel, during the late dear season; and in the wheat-harvest their earnings are such, that, with economy, they may lay by a little for cloaths, rent, and other necessaries, for the winter. It is, probably, owing to the demand for agricultural labour, in the corn parishes, that the population of Seend has rather decreased; and that the Poor often migrate from thence, in search of better wages, and more constant employment.

Very much to their credit, some children managed to climb out of the deprivations of life suffered in a poor Wiltshire village, and make their way in the world. One such was John Britton, who was born at Kington St Michael, near Chippenham (very close to John Aubrey's home), in 1771. He was the fourth of ten children of the village shopkeeper, and at sixteen was apprenticed to work in the cellar of a London tavern. Largely self-taught, he graduated via a solicitor's office to embark on a series of books describing 'the beauties of England' county by county. The volumes on Wiltshire, which appeared in 1801, were the prototype, and the first of no fewer than fifty-seven works on history, architecture and antiquities, which he continued to write until his death in 1857. In his autobiography he recalled his Wiltshire childhood and included the following fox-hunting anecdotes. The first was of special significance to him, since its original publication in a periodical of 1799 brought him his first recognition as an author and set him on the path to a literary career.

During the winter season, the drowsy monotony of 'Our Village' was occasionally awakened from its lethargy by the musical and stimulating cry of the Duke of Beaufort's fox-hounds, or by Sir James Tylney Long's harriers. After the latter I had many a long and tiring run in my boyish days; and on one occasion followed the pack for five hours, without a moment's rest, and was in at the death of a fourth hare. A hearty repast of bread and cheese, with a glass of ale, at a farm-house, made the most delicious meal I ever enjoyed in my life; for I had left home without breakfast, or leave, and was rewarded with a horse-whip on my return. Three events connected with this place, and the chase, may be shortly noticed, as illustrating the amazing cunning of the fox, and as facts which came under my own cognizance. On one occasion, Reynard was closely pressed by the hounds, when he entered a cottage at the bottom of the hill, where all was quiet and apparently secure; and, as the only visible place of refuge, he leaped into a cradle, in which an infant was

sleeping, and crept under the clothes. The mother of the child, who was in the garden, heard the hounds in full cry, near the cottage, and ran in to secure her sleeping infant, when, on lifting up the clothes, she was greeted with a snarl and display of his fine set of teeth from Reynard. The terror of the poor woman may be imagined, but cannot be described. The baby, however, was safe; the huntsman uncradled the fox; the sports were terminated for the day; and the parent's heart palpitated with joy.

On another occasion, I saw a fox approach the village, with the hounds very near to his brush. Reynard leaped on the top of a wall, and descended into a farm-barken [farmyard]. The dogs followed within two minutes, with the huntsman and sportsmen, in close pursuit; but though there were persons very near the spot – though the scent must have been strong – though every house, stable, barn, rick, well, drain, &c. was searched, the fox remained undiscovered. The huntsman took the hounds round the village, to try if any scent could be found, but without effect.

A third fox, whose actions I watched from an eminence, passed through a hedge near one corner of a field, and ran

Sherborne

North Bradley

on the side of another hedge, at right angles with that through which he entered, pursuing a direct line for about 200 or 300 yards, when he made a turn at right angles through a thick hedge, and thus, instead of going into a small brake or copse of underwood, which was the resort of rabbits, and occasionally the haunt of a fox, and which was only one field distant, he tricked the hounds and the huntsmen. When they had passed by, I saw him emerge from the hedge, cross his previous path, and run about a mile to a cover, called Haywood, where he found protection.

The cunning of the fox is proverbial; and the craniologists refer to the formation of its head and the capacity of its skull, as showing that the brains are larger and more capacious, in proportion to the whole animal, than those of any other brute. My grandfather kept a fox, which he had reared from a cub, had tamed it, and made it as docile and domesticated as a dog. It was generally chained to its den, or house; but was occasionally allowed to accompany its master in the fields, and to the parlour of an evening, when the old gentleman amused himself with his glass of gin-toddy, and the everlasting pipe. Reynard's company was however very alarming to me; for, having thrown stones at him in confinement, he often showed his murderous but fine teeth, which warned me against his anger and power. My grandfather was fond of a fox-hunt, and on two occasions allowed his favourite to be turned into an adjoining wood, and hunted by the Duke of Beaufort's hounds. On the first occasion, after a chase of some twenty miles, he made his escape, and returned home the next morning. The second chase was fatal; as the fox was killed after half an hour's run.

Britton, though he derived much of his education from insatiable reading during and after his London apprenticeship, nevertheless had as a child attended various schools in villages around Chippenham. In this respect he was luckier than many of his contemporaries. Village schools offered a glimmer of hope for self-improvement, including – as the vicar and squire saw it – the possibility of higher moral and religious standards. Often it was the incumbent or a Nonconformist minister who took the initiative. The following letters, written by the curate of Netheravon between 1794 and 1796, speak for themselves. They have survived and been published because their author, Sydney Smith, was later to achieve fame as an entertaining essayist, one of the founders of the Edinburgh Review, *and above all as a witty and amiable conversationalist, 'the Smith of Smiths'. The letters are addressed to Mr and Mrs Michael Hicks Beach, of Williamstrip, Gloucestershire, who were lord and lady of the manor of Netheravon.*

Madam

In our conversation about the poor of Netheravon you agreed with me that some of the boys and girls might possibly be prevented from attending church, or the Sunday School from a want of proper clothing, and you were so good as to add, that you would endeavor in some degree to remove this impediment, if it were found to exist. On Sunday last there were 3 or 4 children with their feet upon the cold stones without any shoes, and one came a perfect *Sans culottes* – or at least only with some grinning remnants of that useful garment, just sufficient to shew that he was so clad from necessity, and not from any ingenious Theory he had taken up against such an useful invention. If the Sunday School had begun, I should have imagined that the poor boy thought it his duty to come ready for whipping, as a fowl is sent from the poulterers, trussed and ready for roasting. In whatsoever manner and to whatsoever extent you may chuse to alleviate this species of misery, be so good as to remember that I am on the spot, and shall be happy to carry your benevolent intentions into execution, in the best manner that I am able. – In the mean time Madam I have the honor of being etc., etc.

Sydney Smith

Dear Sr

Upon my return from Bath I began to carry into execution your plan of establishing a Sunday School at

Netheravon. Andrew Goulter whom you mentioned as a man likely to undertake it, is going to quit the place. Bendall the Blacksmith, Harry Cozens, taylor, and Cousin to the Clerk, and Giles Harding have all applied for the appointment. The last I consider as out of the question, his wife cannot read, and he has no room fit to receive the Children. Henry Cozens in my opinion is the most eligible he seems to be the most sensible man of the 2. His wife reads, his Brother reads, and his apprentice reads. He has a good kitchen, some room in his Shop and his mother next door has a good kitchen which may be filled with the overflowings of the School, if it ever should overflow. I have mentioned the Salary you arranged with me to the applicants, viz 2s. per Sunday and 2 Score of faggots.

The Children will attend Xtmas day, and good Friday; is the master to be pd for those days? It is impossible to find 2 Rooms in the same house for boys and girls; if they are put to different houses, the divided Salary will be too small to induce any reputable man to accept it.

The Books that are wanted will be, about 60 Spelling Books (with easy lessons of reading at the end) beginning from the Letters and going on progressing in Syllables; 20 new Testaments and 20 pray'r Books. Miss Hannah More's Books I think you will like very much if you look at them; They are 5s. per 100; if you will send me down 100 of them, I think I can distribute them with effect. The people who had sittings in the great pew have given them up, and Munday is going to fit it up for the children. The people all express a great desire of sending their children to the School. The only farmer I have yet had an opportunity of speaking to, is Farmer Munday; he will contribute with great cheerfulness. I shall talk to the farmers collectively at the Vestry, and individually out of it. . . . A few forms will be wanting for the Sunday School; will you empower me to order them? In the very hot weather why might not the children be instructed in the church before, and after Service, instead of the little hot room in which they would otherwise be stuffed. I shall mention it to the church Wardens with your approbation.

I am just returned from allying the splendid Pyck to the antient house of the Maskelynes. I thought when I turned my Eyes upon the enchanting couple that I was marrying a Baboon to a Sow. however it went off very well, they were very thankful; he was all love and she was all modesty. Nothing can equal the profound, the unmeasur-able, the awful dulness of this place, in the which I lye dead and buried, in hopes of a joyful resurrection in the year 1796. – I am my dear Sr yours sincerely

Sydney Smith

Madam

Immediately upon my arrival from Bath I proceeded to organise your School of Industry. I have selected 1 Girl from every family in the parish, whose poverty entitled them to such releif; they amount to 20. I have set them first of all upon making a coarse canvas bag each, to hold their work in; which bags will be numbered, and hung round the room, when they leave School. We have divided the week between darning, sewing, and knitting; spinning is postponed for the present. I have weighed out the mater-ials to Mr. Bendall, they are entered in a book. I have directed him how to enter the receipt and expenditure of materials, so that you may at any time satisfy yourself of their application. His salary is fixed at 4s. per Week, and firing. I shall attend closely to your new seminary while I stay, and shall before my departure write down, and submit to you, such regulations, as I think conducive to the welfare of that, and the Sunday School. Several little things will be wanting. Will you tell me in your next dispatches to Thomas Turner to what shop at Devizes I am to send for yarn if there should be a deficiency? and where I am to get any prayer books? – of which from the *really surprising* manner in which the children come on under Bendall, there will soon be great need. You have no idea of the emulation that he has inspired them with; all the while

I was at Bath there was not a single child absent. I write these things to you instead of Mr. B. because you have more leisure to attend to them.

I have a great notion that Mr. Astley never received my 2nd letter from Bath, he must have thought my silence very extraordinary, and very impolite. I hope it has reached him by this time. Mr. B. may not have seen the inclosed advertisement. I quit this place in March – I have heard of no successor; a Gentleman Curate called to Day to survey the place, and premises, and galloped away in 2 minutes with ev'ry mark of astonishment, and antipathy. no news; the Dykes all well; the only scandal of the place, that the Widow Rivers is going to be married to one of the Hearnes of the Down Farm. Do not imagine my good madam that this long letter requirs any answer. I only beg you thro' the medium of Thomas Turner to tell me how to get Prayer books and yarn, and I will acquit you of all impoliteness. Pray remember me very kindly to Mr. B. I feel for you both sincerely, may God make those children which remain dutiful and amiable, your pride, and pleasure: and the comfort of your old age.

I have left the bills for the cloathes given to children at the Sunday School, with Thomas Turner. They are considerably within the sum you limited me to. I am happy to have been your Steward but I am going, and therefore, resign my charge.

Smith's evident delight at the prospect of leaving Netheravon brings us round to the more general question of clergymen and their wives. As articulate and educated men and women with, in most cases, an intimate knowledge of their parishioners, they bridge the gulf between the visiting intelligentsia (who, as we have seen, have tended to write poems about rivers or criticize the aesthetics of grazing sheep) and the local residents (who in general have left no record of their views on Wessex life and countryside). Whether the clergy were contented, disgruntled or intrigued by what they observed around them, they certainly proved useful reporters, as we shall see. Life in a remote parish

could be lonely and uncomfortable for them, and these replies to a questionnaire from the Bishop of Salisbury in 1783 serve as a reminder.

Do you constantly reside upon this cure, and in the house belonging to it? If not, where, and at what distance from it, is your usual place of residence? How long in each year are you absent? And what is the reason for such absence?

Rev Thomas Fisher, Bishopstrow

I have constantly resided in my parish and in the house belonging to the rectory till the latter end of the year 1782 to the May following, during which time my health obliged me to make Bath my residence, being so much afflicted with the gout as to disable me from doing the duty of my church; but took particular care to have my church regularly supplied morning and afternoon by a neighbouring clergyman; and the dampness of my situation in the winter, occasioned by the water-meadows that surround me, was another reason for my absence.

Rev Dr George Wells, North Newnton

I reside at the parsonage house of Manningford Bruce. I am seldom, I had almost said never, absent. The parochial clergy are in a manner tied down to a single spot by a multitude of restraints, some of them very irksome and disagreeable to say the least of them. They are precluded from almost every possibility of bettering their condition; being out of the sight of those men who have it in their power to do something for them and with whom some of them have possibly formed connections, they are in consequence out of their minds; and a constant attendance on the duties of their profession like the impotence of the man in the Gospel usually puts it in the power of some other person to step before them.

Chapmanslade

Portland

Chiswell, Portland

Lyme Regis

Rev Thomas Meyler, Preshute

The house belonging to the vicar of Preshute having been destroyed by fire in, or shortly before, the year 1607, and never since rebuilt, I constantly reside at the parsonage house of Marlborough St Peter's, not half a mile from Preshute church; and as the last and present incumbents have enjoyed both benefices, it is to be wished that all future bishops will confer them on one and the same person, as one will furnish him with bread and cheese, and the other with a place to eat and sleep.

Rev Peter Brodie, Winterslow

I think myself justified in saying constantly. I have been rector 16 years. I had no house. I bought one (the nearest to the church) where I spent most of my time. I built a new house. I have lived in it these 8 years. I have never been absent more than a month at a time, and that was but once, and for the benefit of sea bathing. I have business which calls me to London sometimes, but I am seldom absent a fortnight together.

Rev Dr John Eyre, Wylye

Yes, never absent, only one Sunday in almost three and twenty years.

Bath, influential society, sea-bathing. So these seem to have been the bored and neglected Wiltshire clergyman's daydreams. In Dorset civilization was closer at hand. Weymouth and Lyme Regis developed into seaside resorts during the 1780s, the former attracting the king and his retinue (and a host of aspiring 'royal-watchers'), the latter appealing to a more select company, who disapproved of the Weymouth razzmatazz. Jane Austen visited Lyme, and described the scene during the 1804 season in a letter to her sister, a world which she immortalized in SENSE AND SENSIBILITY, published in 1811.

My dear Cassandra

I take the first sheet of this fine striped paper to thank you for your letter from Weymouth, and express my hopes of your being at Ibthrop before this time. I expect to hear that you reached it yesterday evening, being able to get as far as Blandford on Wednesday. Your account of Weymouth contains nothing which strikes me so forcibly as there being no ice in the town. For every other vexation I was in some measure prepared, and particularly for your disappointment in not seeing the Royal Family go on board on Tuesday, having already heard from Mr. Crawford that he had seen you in the very act of being too late, but for there being no ice what could prepare me? Weymouth is altogether a shocking place, I perceive, without recommendation of any kind, and worthy only of being frequented by the inhabitants of Gloucester. I am really very glad that we did not go there, and that Henry and Eliza saw nothing in it to make them feel differently. You found my letter at Andover, I hope, yesterday, and have now for many hours been satisfied that your kind anxiety on my behalf was as much thrown away as kind anxiety usually is. I continue quite well; in proof of which I have bathed again this morning. It was absolutely necessary that I should have the little fever and indisposition which I had: it has been all the fashion this week in Lyme. Miss Anna Cove was confined for a day or two and her Mother thinks she was saved only by a timely Emetic (prescribed by Dr. Robinson) from a serious illness and Miss Bonham has been under Mr. Carpenter's care for several days with a sort of nervous fever, and tho' she is now well enough to walk abroad she is still very tall and does not come to the Rooms. We all of us attended them both on Wednesday evening and last evening I suppose I must say or Martha will think Mr. Peter Debary slighted. My mother had her pool of commerce each night and divided the first with Le Chevalier, who was lucky enough to divide the other with somebody else. I hope he will always win enough to empower him to treat himself with so great an indulgence

Golden Cap

Near Kimmeridge Bay

as cards must be to him. He enquired particularly after you, not being aware of your departure. We are quite settled in our Lodgings by this time as you may suppose, and everything goes on in the usual order. The servants behave very well, and make no difficulties, tho' nothing certainly can exceed the inconvenience of the offices, except the general dirtiness of the house and furniture and all its inhabitants. Hitherto the weather has been just what we could wish – the continuance of the dry season is very necessary to our comfort. I endeavour as far as I can to supply your place and be useful, and keep things in order. I detect dirt in the water-decanter as fast as I can and give the Cook physic which she throws off her stomach. I forget whether she used to do this, under your administration. James is the delight of our lives, he is quite an uncle Toby's annuity to us. My mother's shoes were never so well blacked before, and our plate never looked so clean. He waits extremely well, is attentive, handy, quick and quiet, and in short has a great many more than all the cardinal virtues (for the cardinal virtues in themselves have been so often possessed that they are no longer worth having) and amongst the rest, that of wishing to go to Bath, as I understand from Jenny. He has the laudable thirst I fancy for travelling, which in poor James Selby was so much reprobated; and part of his disappointment in not going with his master, arose from his wish of seeing London. . . . I have written to Buller and I have written to Mr. Pyne, on the subject of the broken lid; it was valued by Anning here we were told at five shillings, and as that appeared to us beyond the value of all the furniture in the room together, we have referred ourselves to the owner. The Ball last night was pleasant, but not full for Thursday. My father staid very contentedly till half-past nine (we went a little after eight), and then walked home with James and a lanthorn, though I believe the lanthorn was not lit, as the moon was up; but this lanthorn may sometimes be a great convenience to him. My mother and I staid about an hour later. Nobody asked me the first two dances; the two next I danced with Mr. Crawford, and had I chosen to stay longer might have danced with Mr. Granville, Mrs. Granville's son, whom my dear friend Miss Armstrong offered to introduce to me, or with a new odd-looking man who had been eyeing me for some time, and at last, without any introduction, asked me if I meant to dance again. I think he must be Irish by his ease, and because I imagine him to belong to the hon'ble Barnwalls, who are the son, and son's wife of an Irish viscount, bold queer-looking people, just fit to be quality at Lyme. Mrs. Fraser and the Schuylers went away – I do not know where – last Tuesday for some days and when they return the Schuylers I understand are to remain here a very little while longer. I called yesterday morning (ought it not in strict propriety to be termed yester-morning?) on Miss Armstrong and was introduced to her father and mother. Like other young ladies she is considerably genteeler than her parents. Mrs. Armstrong sat darning a pair of stockings the whole of my visit. But I do not mention this at home, lest a warning should act as an example. We afterwards walked together for an hour on the Cobb; she is very converseable in a common way; I do not perceive wit or genius, but she has sense and some degree of taste, and her manners are very engaging. She seems to like people rather too easily. She thought the Downes pleasant etc etc. I have seen nothing of Mr. and Mrs. Manhood. My aunt mentions Mrs. Holder's being returned from Cheltenham so her summer ends before theirs begins. Hooper was heard of well at the Madeiras. Eliza would envy him. I hope Martha thinks you looking better than when she saw you in Bath. Jenny has fastened up my hair to-day in the same manner that she used to do up Miss Lloyd's – which makes us both very happy. I need not say that we are particularly anxious for your next letter to know how you find Mrs. Lloyd and Martha. Say everything kind for us to the latter. The former I fear must be beyond any remembrance of or from the absent.

Yrs. affect'ly

J.A.

Weymouth

Friday Evening. The bathing was so delightful this morning and Molly so pressing with me to enjoy myself that I believe I staid in rather too long, as since the middle of the day I have felt unreasonably tired. I shall be more careful another time, and shall not bathe to-morrow as I had before intended. Jenny and James are walked to Charmouth this afternoon. I am glad to have such an amusement for him, as I am very anxious for his being at once quiet and happy. He can read, and I must get him some books. Unfortunately he has read the 1st vol. of *Robinson Crusoe*. We have the Pinckards newspaper however which I shall take care to lend him.

Daniel Defoe would not have approved of such sophistication at Lyme, but then Miss Austen did not approve of her servants reading Robinson Crusoe. *And she certainly did not approve of Weymouth, 'altogether a shocking place'. There were too many people of the wrong sort, and too much vulgar gaiety. To the eye of an impressionable schoolgirl, however, the Weymouth season was a scene of great excitement. Here are the reminiscences of Elizabeth Ham, who grew up in and around the resort.*

The great plague of the place was the 'Season' to all sober Housewives. Our country connection was large, and no sooner was the King come than country Cousins came too. The influx of visitors at such times was very great. The Continent was quite shut to the British idler, and Weymouth was all the fashion. Every house and every room that could be procured was engaged. Every day something was going on to amuse the King. This, no doubt, was done with a motive. There was in general either a Public Breakfast, a Review, or a Sail, for the morning, and the Play in the evening four times a week. Tuesdays and Fridays were Ball nights, but the Royal Family did not attend these. On Sunday evenings the rooms were open for Tea and Promenade. This the King never missed. A cord was stretched from the Ball-room door to the Tea-room, or rather Card-room, where the Royal Family took their tea. They were met in the Lobby by the Master of Ceremonies, Mr. Rodber, with a candle in each hand, who walked backward before them, up the stairs and into the Ball-room, where all those who had the *entrée* were standing within the cord. His Majesty was generally dragging the Queen behind him with one hand, bowing his head slowly, and speaking fast to those within the cord, whilst she ducked and smiled and spoke according to the time allowed her. The Princesses followed according to age, and had their say in turn. It generally took from three quarters to an hour to make this short transit. The cord was then removed, but the door was always left open where their Majesties and their invited guests were taking their tea.

At the Public Breakfasts Marquees were generally pitched in some chosen spot and a platform laid for Dancing. The Public were permitted to go and look at the Breakfast before hand, and to stand near enough to see the eating and dancing, one side of the Marquee being generally open, and His Majesty's loving subjects could enjoy the satisfaction of seeing their beloved Monarch draw a Drum-stick through his teeth, in which he seemed to delight, and hearing his call for 'Buttered Peas', and 'Moneymusk' to set the dancers in motion. Country Dances were the only ones then in vogue, but the Princesses never joined in them on these occasions.

Once a week the Royal party generally went for a sail. The Royal Yachts were in attendance for this purpose. There were three Frigates lying in the Roads for protection. These always accompanied the Royal Yachts. The King never seemed afraid of weather. The Queen and Princesses always wore dark blue Habits on these occasions, and I have often seen them look very miserable and bedraggled on their return.

There were frequent Reviews, but not weekly, for the waste of life and powder was to be considered. I do not know if this was much thought of.

With all this gaiety going on, it was no wonder that all

Looking west to Portland from Flower's Barrow fort

Swanage

Eype

who could flocked to Weymouth. It was no unusual thing to see a Chaise stop at the door, and three ladies with all their luggage descend, and hope that they should not put Mrs. Ham to any inconvenience, that they could make *one* bed do if that was all etc. etc., and this from people with whom we had but the slightest acquaintance. All this made my mother desperate, and she thought she would try what effect letting two of her rooms would produce. This she never did after I left school, but I remember one Summer we had General Goldsworthy, one of the King's Equerries, in the house, and another, Major Pye, brother to the Poet Laureate.

I conclude my mother used to be tired of going about with her visitors, for I very often went in her place, and when Major Pye was in our house, he used to find me out and assist the party I was with to good places.

That year there was a rural fete given on Maiden Castle, a British Camp, close to Monkton where my uncle resided. I went to stay a few days at his house at this time. We walked, a party of us, to the ground. Every regiment had a marquee pitched, with refreshments. The sports were: grinning through a horse-collar, jumping in sacks, catching a pig by the tail, which said tail had been previously shaved and greased, donkey racing, the last donkey to be the winner; rolls dipped in treacle suspended by strings to be devoured by boys with their hands tied behind them; diving for apples in a meal-tub; *Le mat du Coc* [greasy pole?]; women racing for under garments, with other rural sports made Royal for the occasion.

The year of Cassandra Austen's visit to Weymouth, 1804, was also remembered by Elizabeth Ham, but not for its gaiety.

Old Mr. Mansell and my brother John happened to be with us, when one morning very early the latter came and tapped at, my father's door, which was close to mine, to tell him the French Fleet was off the coast. This I heard, and immediately began to dress. Mr. Mansell was dis-turbed by the noise and opening his door called out, 'What's the matter, John?' 'The French are landing in the West Bay,' he replied. 'Oh, d—m 'em; let's be at 'em,' said the old man hurrying on his clothes.

In a few minutes Drums were beating to arms. Officers galloping about in all directions. The horses being put to the Royal Carriages, and everybody standing at their doors asking everybody for news. I was soon dressed and down, and the first person I encountered was the servant girl with the sweeping brush in her hand hurrying to the front door. 'Where are you going, Sally?' said I. 'Oh, Miss Bessy, I am going away, I won't stop a minute longer!' 'Well put down the brush first,' said I, 'you need not take that with you at all events.' Seeing me take it so cooly, she paused a little to consider. The next minute Mary appeared, then a slip of a girl about twelve, with her bonnet and cloak on and her gloves in her hand. 'How are we to go, Bessy? Why don't you get ready?' The next minute Frederick Mansell who with his wife was staying with a family near, came across to ask for a place for his wife, supposing we should harness old Jewel to the Cart, well knowing that no conveyance could be hired.

Nothing more was known all this time but that under cover of a dense fog, the French were landing somewhere. That there was real cause for alarm no one could doubt, who witnessed the anxious looks of the hurrying Field Officers, and saw the Royal Carriages drawn up in front of Gloster Lodge, ready to start at a moment's notice. Still the fog hung its dense veil over the threatened mischief, and mystery and suspense added ten-fold force to the alarm. All that could be learnt was this. Soon after dawn some Portland fishermen had landed on that Island with the report that having been out looking after their nets they were lost in the fog. When all at once they found themselves in the midst of a large Fleet of armed ships. They pulled with all their might, and it was fortunately towards land. A certain Mr. Daniel who had recently purchased some stone-quarries in the Island, was awakened, and taking horse galloped to the Ferry and brought the news to Weymouth, declaring that the shots were making the pebbles fly about him as he rode along Chessel bank. Of course there were Sentinels stationed along the shore but as there was no attempt to land on that part up to nine or ten o'clock it was concluded that the Enemy was trying some other part of the Coast.

By this time troops of Yeomanry were galloping into the Town. Everybody still at their doors asking everybody for further news. About twelve o'clock the fog thought proper to lift up its awful curtain and to disclose to all eager eyes strained seaward, first the frigates and Royal Yachts with sails all set and ready for action, then a clear expanse of smooth unruffled water without another speck of canvas in sight. The French Fleet had vanished, 'and like the baseless fabric of a vision left not a wreck behind'. Poor Mr. Daniel hid himself behind his Portland Stone for weeks after.

The Weymouth of Elizabeth Ham is best known as the 'Budmouth' of Thomas Hardy's THE TRUMPET MAJOR, although her reminiscences, which were not published until 1945, could not have been known to the novelist. In this short extract Hardy's heroine, Anne Garland, makes her way from Weymouth across to Portland in the hope of catching a glimpse of HMS Victory, on which Bob Loveday, her sweetheart, is a sailor.

The morrow was market-day at the seaport, and in this she saw her opportunity. A carrier went from Overcombe at six o'clock thither, and having to do a little shopping for herself she gave it as a reason for her intended day's absence, and took a place in the van. When she reached the town it was still early morning, but the borough was already in the zenith of its daily bustle and show. The King was always out-of-doors by six o'clock, and such cock-crow hours at Gloucester Lodge produced an equally forward 'stir among the population. She alighted, and passed down the esplanade, as fully thronged by persons of fashion at this time of mist and level sunlight as a watering-place in the present day is at four in the afternoon. Dashing bucks and beaux in cocked hats, black feathers, ruffles, and frills, stared at her as she hurried along; the beach was swarming with bathing women, wearing waistbands that bore the national refrain, 'God save the King,' in gilt letters; the shops were all open, and Sergeant Stanner, with his sword-stuck bank-notes and heroic gaze, was beating up at two guineas and a crown, the crown to drink his Majesty's health.

She soon finished her shopping, and then, crossing over into the old town, pursued her way along the coast-road to Portland. At the end of an hour she had been rowed across the Fleet (which then lacked the convenience of a bridge), and reached the base of Portland Hill. The steep incline before her was dotted with houses, showing the pleasant peculiarity of one man's doorstep being behind his neighbour's chimney, and slabs of stone as the common material for walls, roof, floor, pig-sty, stable-manger, door-scraper, and garden-stile. Anne gained the summit, and followed along the central track over the huge lump of freestone which forms the peninsula, the wide sea prospect extending as she went on. Weary with her journey, she approached the extreme southerly peak of rock, and gazed from the cliff at Portland Bill, or Beal, as it was in those days more correctly called.

The wild, herbless, weather-worn promontory was quite a solitude, and, saving the one old lighthouse about fifty yards up the slope, scarce a mark was visible to show that humanity had ever been near the spot. Anne found herself a seat on a stone, and swept with her eyes the tremulous expanse of water around her that seemed to utter a ceaseless unintelligible incantation. Out of the three hundred and sixty degrees of her complete horizon two hundred and fifty were covered by waves, the *coup d'oeil* including the area of troubled waters known as the Race, where two seas meet to effect the destruction of such vessels as could not be mastered by one. She counted the

Weymouth Sands

The Crown, Everleigh

craft within her view: there were five; no, there were only four; no, there were seven, some of the specks having resolved themselves into two. They were all small coasters, and kept well within sight of land.

The plight of ordinary men and women, acting out 'dramas of a grandeur and unity truly Sophoclean' against a backcloth of the Wessex countryside, is the theme underlying all the variations of Hardy's output, and the hallmark of his genius. His was a retrospective vision, a nostalgic evocation of the Dorset of his childhood which has become familiar to millions through his matchless power of description.

But Hardy's was not the only voice raised in defence of the Wessex labourer. The degradation caused by poverty, which grew progressively worse as the Napoleonic Wars pushed up prices, had been placed in the public arena by the work of Eden and others, and the labouring poor were to find vociferous new champions among the reforming politicians of the early nineteenth century. William Cobbett, riding through Wiltshire in 1826, was forthright and dire.

In taking my leave of this beautiful vale I have to express my deep shame, as an Englishman, at beholding the general *extreme poverty* of those who cause this vale to produce such quantities of food and raiment. This is, I verily believe it, the *worst used labouring people upon the face of the earth*. Dogs and hogs and horses are treated with *more civility*; and as to food and lodging, how gladly would the labourers change with them! This state of things never can continue many years! *By some means or other* there must be an end to it; and my firm belief is, that that end will be dreadful. In the mean while I see, and I see it with pleasure, that the common people *know that they are ill used*; and that they cordially, most cordially, hate those who ill-treat them.

A neat illustration of this rather chilling remark is provided by another fox-hunting story, which supposedly occurred in the 1870s.

Some years ago, when the late Sir Richard Glynn was master of the renowned Blackmoor Vale Fox Hounds, they met at a place called Totnall corner, near Leigh. They drew a wood named the Castles; it turned a very bad day for scent. A lad told one of the Whips that he saw a fox break away and run across a field towards an old man hedging but the hounds failed to follow the line. The Whip galloped the field to ask the old man if he had seen the fox. The old chap stammered very badly, and the following conversation took place:

Whip 'Have you seen the fox, my man?
Old Man 'What is'er lik-lik-lik-like, ser?'
W. 'Surely you know what a fox is like?'
O.M. 'Have 'er g-g-got a b-b-brishy ta-ta-tail, ser?'
W. 'Yes' (rather impatiently), 'have you seen it?'
O.M. 'Did 'er 'ave a white ti-ti-tip to his tail, ser?'
W. 'Yes, yes.'
O.M. 'Did 'er 'ave to-to-two lit-little p-p-pricked up ears, ser?'
W. (Getting a bit cross) 'Yes.'
O.M. 'Did 'er 'ave a sh-sh-sh-sharp no-no-nose, ser?'
W. 'Yes' (quite angrily) 'have you seen it?'
O.M. 'I ha-ha-haven't zeed no-no-nothing o-o-ou'n, ser.'
W. 'Dam you!'
O.M. (A little hard of hearing) 'Sa-sa-same to you, s-ser.'

But back to Cobbett. He was a perceptive traveller, indignant and enthusiastic by turns. Here he is, about to set off on his famous journey down the valley of the Avon in 1826, extolling the virtues of the Crown Inn at Everleigh on Salisbury Plain.

This inn is one of the nicest, and, in summer, one of the pleasantest, in England; for, I think, that my experience in this way will justify me in speaking thus positively. The house is large, the yard and the stables good, the landlord a

Marlborough Downs

farmer also, and, therefore, no cribbing your horses in hay or straw and yourself in eggs and cream. The garden, which adjoins the south side of the house, is large, of good shape, has a terrace on one side, lies on the slope, consists of well-disposed clumps of shrubs and flowers, and of short-grass very neatly kept. In the lower part of the garden there are high trees, and, amongst these, the tulip-tree and the live-oak. Beyond the garden is a large clump of lofty sycamores, and in these a most populous rookery, in which, of all things in the world, I delight. The village, which contains 301 souls, lies to the north of the inn, but adjoining its premises. All the rest, in every direction, is bare down or open arable. I am now sitting at one of the southern windows of this inn, looking across the garden towards the rookery. It is nearly sun-setting; the rooks are skimming and curving over the tops of the trees; while, under the branches, I see a flock of several hundred sheep, coming nibbling their way in from the Down, and going to their fold.

One of the farms which Cobbett must have passed on his ride down the Avon valley was Widdington, near Upavon. Here, some fifty years earlier, Henry Hunt, his friend and fellow-spokesman on behalf of the poor, had been born. Hunt is best remembered as the speaker at the meeting in Manchester in 1819 which resulted in the Peterloo massacre. He was of Wiltshire yeoman stock, and when, as a prisoner in Ilchester gaol from 1820 to 1822, he came to write his memoirs, he recorded at great length his petulant but privileged early life as a farmer's son, before he began his political career. Here he describes his wedding in 1796 to a daughter of the landlord of the Bear Inn at Devizes.

My father took the first opportunity of telling me that, as I was determined to marry against his will, he should do but little for me, compared to what he would have done if I had married to please him. He would, he said, give me, or rather he would lend me, the stock upon Widdington farm, and I might begin to furnish my house as soon as I pleased; but I must do this out of the fortune which I was to have with my wife. There was a most excellent stock upon this farm, the rent of which was three hundred pounds a year. There were fifteen or sixteen hundred of the finest Southdown sheep, the very best in the county, as this was a fine sheep farm, in fact, principally so; twelve cows; six most valuable cart horses, and all other live and dead stock complete. With this arrangement I was perfectly content, and indeed it was much better than I had any reason to expect. The farm was, in reality, a very beautiful one, with a very good house, and all necessary appendages attached to it. I now seemed to be in a fair way of obtaining the height of my ambition. This happy intelligence I lost no time in communicating to the family at Devizes, and the necessary orders for furniture, etc. were given without delay. I left it all to the lady, as it was to be paid for out of her fortune. Few young men entered into life with fairer prospects in the farming line; very few farmers in the county had such a stock of all sorts; in truth, nothing was wanting.

The happy day at length arrived. It was the twelfth of January. My sister, who was to be one of the bride-maids, and my friend the clergyman of Enford, who was to marry us, went over in a chaise to Devizes the evening before. Upon retiring to rest, having undressed myself, I sat down in an easy chair, meditating upon the serious engagement into which I was to enter on the morrow. In this situation I fell fast asleep, and did not awake until three o'clock in the morning, when I had caught a dreadful cold, and was in a shivering fit, which I could not get rid of till I arose in the morning. I was excessively ill the whole of the day. We were taken to the church in a post coach, and being married we returned to breakfast, where a large party was assembled to greet us. We were engaged to dine at the Castle, at Marlborough, which Inn was kept by my wife's brother. We, the married couple, in a chaise, and two post coaches, each with four beautiful grey horses, with the rest of the party, accordingly set out to

Marlborough, where we spent the day, during the whole of which I suffered great pain, being all the time extremely ill. We returned to Devizes to tea, after taking which we were to go home to Widdington. Just as we were about to start, Mr. Halcombe took me aside with his son into the next room, and holding out a canvass bag, he said, 'here, my son, is all that I can afford to give you with my daughter. In this bag is a thousand pounds. I wish it were ten times as much; but, such as it is, may God grant you to enjoy it! I have no doubt but it will wear well, as it was got honestly.'

This again was more than I expected, as the only time I had ever permitted him to speak about money, the old gentleman hinted at no more than five hundred pounds; but I believe my father had said something which made him double the sum. I thanked him most heartily; not forgetting to add, that his daughter was the prize at which I had aimed, and not the money. He replied, that he should give his other daughter the same, without trenching upon what he meant to give his sons. . . .

We now set off in a coach towards our future residence, Widdington Farm, a distance of ten miles. The company consisted of myself, the bride, her sister and mine, who were the two bride-maids, and the clergyman. I had, by this time, completely recovered from the effect of my cold; but, what was rather remarkable, before we had accomplished half our journey, we discovered that the bride had suddenly lost her voice, without feeling any pain or illness. So completely had she lost it, that she could not articulate a single syllable, otherwise than in a whisper. I was very much alarmed at first, but as she assured us it was only a cold, and that she felt not the least pain or uneasiness whatever; and as, with perfect good humour, she congratulated me on being about to take to my home 'a quiet wife', the alarm gradually passed off.

Widdington Farm lies about a mile from the turnpike road, and when the carriage turned out of the high road I was obliged, as it was dark, to get on the coach box to direct the post boys; and, after considerable difficulty, we reached the house; it being a road over which a chaise probably had not passed since my father left the farm, twenty years before this period. Although every thing was prepared comfortably for our reception, yet a lone farm, in a valley upon the downs, which compose Salisbury Plain, and not a house within a mile, was quite a different thing from the cheerful scenes to which Mrs. Hunt and her sister had been accustomed. A deep silence reigned around; not a tree nor even a bush was to be seen; and, since we left the turnpike road, the carriage having passed over the turf for nearly the last mile, the well-known sound of wheels rattling over the stones had never once vibrated upon the ears of those who were so much accustomed to it; altogether, it was so very different from every thing to which the ladies had ever before been habituated, that, even after I had introduced them into the parlour, which was well lighted up, and where the hospitable board seemed almost to invite their welcome, yet I could see that Miss Halcombe looked at her sister almost in a state of despondency, as much as to say, 'God of Heaven! what enchanted castle are we come to at last?' However, when we were once seated round the table, with the door closed, the solitary gloom speedily vanished, for we soon made it appear that there was as much cheerfulness to be obtained in a lone farm house as there was in one of the most public and best frequented inns upon the Bath road. Miss Halcombe, as a matter of delicacy, had always declined to see this residence before she was married, notwithstanding I had repeatedly pressed her to ride over and give orders about the arrangement of the house, and other domestic affairs.

During the first fortnight that we were married, my wife never spoke one word louder than a whisper. At the end of that time her voice returned, to the great joy of myself and all her friends. The honey-moon passed with uninterrupted felicity; in fact it was a honey-moon all the year round, and we were blessed with an endearing pledge

The Marlborough Downs, near Rockley

Stubble burning, Little Bedwyn

of our loves before the honey-moon appeared even in its wane. Nearly a year had now gone by in one unbroken scene of pleasure and gay delight. My wife was of a cheerful disposition, and fond of company, in which I most cordially participated, and consequently we were seldom without plenty of visitors. As soon as we were married I purchased two more horses and a gig; thus my establishment at once consisted of three horses and a gig, and when to these are added grey-hounds and pointers etc. etc. the reader will perceive that I cut a dashing figure, whether at home, at the table, in the field, or on the road. I drove two thorough-bred mares in a tandem, with which I could and did accomplish, in a trot, fourteen miles within the hour; I was almost always the first in the chase, having become a subscriber to a pack of hounds; and my pointers were as well bred, and as well broken, as any sportsman's in the county.

Discontent among farm labourers at what they saw as the callous attitude of their employers, the gentlemen farmers to whose lifestyle Hunt had once aspired, eventually boiled over, as Cobbett predicted. In the late autumn of 1830 a wave of rick-burning and machine-breaking swept across southern England, inspired by a legendary figure, 'Captain Swing'. The course of this uprising through Wessex was erratic and brief, but while it lasted it engendered a climate of fear and panic which had probably not been felt since the false alarm at Weymouth a generation earlier.

For an eye-witness account of the events in one village, Alton Barnes in Pewsey Vale, we are indebted to Maria Hare, wife of the rector. Her husband, Augustus Hare, had been appointed to the living during the previous year, and the recently married couple were settling down to what they envisaged would be a quiet life in their remote parish. Sadly, Augustus died in 1834.

We have had no further alarm beyond the many reports, of which, if we believed one half, one could not have much rest. However, at Pewsey there has been a meeting.

Col. Wroughton says the people are satisfied, and there will be one at Devizes to-day. Troops are at Marlborough and Devizes. We have our own special constables, patrols, and fire-engine, and I trust are in a better state of preparation than we were. Poor Mr. Pile is not out of danger, I fear, though I hope he will do well. A large fire-ball was found in his field the morning after the attack. We hear of five great fires over the hills towards Calne, and at Salisbury dreadful work is going on. Our ringleaders are chiefly taken, and we had the pleasure of seeing some of them go past with the cavalry yesterday morning. All the villages round us seem to have contributed their share of men; and I fear there are some very bad ones amongst them. Our village had not one, and only two were from Great Alton, but of course they all rejoice secretly at what is to bring them greater wages. At the same time they are frightened to death, and the wives come crying about their husbands, – they are sure they will get their heads broken, etc. At all hours people are coming, – farmers to consult about what should be done, and with fresh stories. In short, we live in a strange, nervous state; and if we do not make an example, and that speedily, of some of the worst, there will be no end to these outrages.

On Tuesday evening, when all was over, and our fears for the night were quieted by the arrival of the cavalry, Augustus and I sat each in our arm-chair, so completely worn out by the anxiety and fatigue of the day, that we neither of us uttered a word for a couple of hours. From my station at the drawing-room window, I saw the whole combat, and you may guess my horror when, hearing the confusion of Mr. Pile's fall, I saw Augustus rush towards the place, surrounded by the 'bull-dogs', – and my subsequent joy when I saw him get away and walk home. They threatened vengeance so loudly that he kept out of sight from that time, and I talked to the people who came to the door. As soon as they had filed off across the field to Mr. Miller's, I went down to Mr. Pile's, and such a state of distraction as the house presented I never saw. I went again

Alton Barnes

to hear the doctor's report. The sisters were all activity, and busied about their brother, whilst the poor old mother, not allowed to go into the room, went moaning about, lamenting first over her son, and then over her china; she herself got a great blow from one of the iron crows. The greater part of our rioters are men who earn from twelve to twenty shillings a week at the Wharf, and spend it all at the beer-shops. . . .

I have written so confusedly before that I think you will have no clear idea of my share of the day, so I will tell what I saw. On the approach of the troop, as they came over the bridge, Augustus said to me, 'Go home, and keep in the house'; and so amid the cook's entreaties that 'Master would come too', which I knew was vain, we betook ourselves to the house, locked and bolted doors and windows, and had just retreated up-stairs, when a thundering knock came at the front door. Finding my plan of concealment would not do, I presented myself at the drawing-room window, and held a parley with them. 'They wanted to do no harm.' 'What have you got those clubs and hammers for, then?' I refused money and went away, but the continued knocking, and threats of breaking doors and windows, soon made me pull out some shillings and throw to them, with which they went away content. Meanwhile I saw in the churchyard all the women and children collected: leaning over the wall of Mr. Pile's yard I could distinguish Augustus and one or two others; and in the farmyard and all round it were the mob, with shouts, hammering the machine to pieces. I suppose this had gone on for twenty minutes or half an hour, when we (the cook and myself, for the other servants were all gone nearer the scene of the action) heard a tremendous gallop, and in an instant saw Mr. Pile ride furiously amongst the mob, who gave way directly, and had he kept his ground there, all had been well. There was a confusion, and all I could distinguish was that the farmyard was cleared; a report of a gun came from the ricks behind the barns, there was a great scream set up, loud shouts, and to my horror I saw

Augustus and those with him rush into the field amongst them. However, the alarm for him was not long; after a few minutes I distinguished him leaving the crowd, and making his way to the house, and never did my legs carry me more willingly than as I flew down-stairs to open him the door. When I again got to my station, the mob were all come round and advancing upon the Piles' house, and the noise was terrible of breaking their windows and doors. As they had vowed vengeance against Augustus for having brought the gun out of the house, he kept out of sight, whilst I sent away the few who came for money, and who were easily contented. After they had completed their destruction at Mr. Pile's, which was not till the poor mangled victim was brought down-stairs again, and had given them £10, we had the satisfaction of seeing them file away across the fields to Great Alton. In about half an hour they returned to break the Crowe's machine which we had put in the field, and then we saw no more of them; but as they went off to Stanton, declaring their intention of returning at night, it was an amazing relief when Mr. G. and some other men arrived, who said they had just left Devizes, and heard the troops ordered 'on Alton'. And so ended our siege, which it must be owned was as little resisted as ever enemy was; but the best labourers were all at a distance, and those near, far too much frightened to give any help. . . .

The odd thing about the riots is, that this is not a year of scarcity. There has been no hard winter and no uncommon pressure of any sort to raise this outcry. And when one sees that half of the discontented are men who spend their money at the beer-shops, and who might get ample if they chose, it rather hardens one against sympathy with their distress, and inclines one to think the lenity and indulgence granted in return for their proceedings, not the best-judged.

The fury of 1830 achieved little or nothing beyond bitterness and recrimination. Twenty years later, as part of a survey of

English agriculture commissioned by The Times, *Sir James Caird reported that conditions in much of Wiltshire were as bad as ever.*

The wages of labour are lower on Salisbury Plain than in Dorsetshire, and lower than in the dairy and arable districts of North Wilts. An explanation of this may partly be found in the fact, that the command of wages is altogether under the control of the large farmers, some of whom employ the whole labour of a parish. Six shillings a-week was the amount given for ordinary labourers by the most extensive farmer in South Wilts, who holds nearly 5000 acres of land, great part of which is his own property; 7s., however, is the more common rate, and out of that the labourer has to pay 1s. a-week for the rent of his cottage. If prices continue low, it is said that even these wages must be reduced. Where a man's family can earn something at out-door work, this pittance is eked out a little, but in cases where there is a numerous young family, great pinching must be endured. We were curious to know how the money was economised, and hear from a labourer the following account of a day's diet. After doing up his horses he takes breakfast, which is made of flour with a little butter, and water 'from the tea-kettle' poured over it. He takes with him to the field a piece of bread and (if he has not a young family, and can afford it) cheese to eat at mid-day. He returns home in the afternoon to a few potatoes, and possibly a little bacon, though only those who are better off can afford this. The supper very commonly consists of bread and water. The appearance of the labourers showed, as might be expected from such meagre diet, a want of that vigour and activity which mark the well-fed ploughmen of the northern and midland counties. Beer is given by the master in hay-time and harvest. Some farmers allow ground for planting potatoes to their labourers, and carry home their fuel - which, on the downs, where there is no wood, is a very expensive article in a labourer's family.

Both farmers and labourers suffer in this locality from the present over-supply of labour. The farmer is compelled to employ more men than his present mode of operations require, and, to save himself, he pays them a lower rate of wages than is sufficient to give that amount of physical power which is necessary for the performance of a fair day's work. His labour is, therefore, really more costly than where sufficient wages are paid; and, accordingly, in all cases where task-work is done, the rates are higher here than in other counties in which the general condition of the labourer is better. We found a prevalent desire for emigration among the labourers themselves, as their only mode of benefitting those who go and those who remain behind.

Agricultural improvement and the introduction of labour-saving machinery were widely regarded as the villains of the piece. In farming, as in everything else, the Victorians applied scientific principle in the pursuit of progress, sometimes to an alarming degree. Caird's description of a mechanized Dorset farm in 1850 is redolent of modern 'factory-farming' methods.

Dorset village shop

Mere

The West Farm, about a mile from Sutton Waldron, is the first on which Mr. Huxtable commenced his improvements. . . . This is strictly a breeding farm, keeping a stock of milch cows, the calves of which, when reared, are removed to the Hill Farm to be fattened. There is nothing peculiar about the management of the stock here which will not be detailed in the description of the Hill Farm, so that it is only necessary to call attention to the plan adopted by Mr. Huxtable for the cheap distribution of liquid manure over the different divisions of this farm. The whole liquid is carefully collected in a series of tanks, from the lowest of which it is discharged as required, by a force-pump, into pipes, which carry it to the several fields in succession. The pipes are of well-burnt clay, an inch thick, their joints secured with cement. They cost 7d. a yard, and inclusive of an upright discharge column every 200 yards, will not exceed £1 an acre. The pipes and columns are now laid down for the accommodation of 60 acres of the West Farm. When it is requisite to apply the liquid to any portion of these 60 acres, the force-pump is set to work, and a stop put on the discharge column nearest the place to be watered. A hose is then attached to the column and carried into a tub placed on a light broad-wheeled water-cart, which, as soon as filled, is drawn off, and another of the same kind put in its place. The first is then emptied by a man with a bucket, who scatters its contents over the land. By the time he has emptied the first tub the second is full, and he repeats the same process with its contents, and so on, the man at the forcing-pump being thus enabled to deliver a continuous stream of manure at the distance of many hundred yards. . . .

The Hill Farm is the most interesting, for here Mr. Huxtable has most elaborately carried his science into practice. A few years ago this was an open chalk down; it is bare and barren, high and windy, rising abruptly from the adjoining vale to an elevation of 500 feet. . . . The farm consists of 280 acres of land, all of which bear every year alternate crops of corn and cattle food. . . . Implements of every kind for economising and perfecting labour are in requisition – cultivators, scarifiers, clodcrushers, seed-drills, dibbling machines, and liquid-manure-and-seed drill.

At this season the operations on the land are not so interesting as those going on in the buildings – the meat and manure factory of the farm. . . . They are constructed with a strict eye to economy, both of expense and labour; and there is not a nook about them which the critical eye will discover as either unnecessary or very inconveniently situated. The whole stock of the farm, except the breeding ewes, are kept constantly housed night and day, summer and winter, and no particle of their food or manure is suffered to be wasted.

Beginning our description with the steam-engine: it thrashes and winnows the corn, cuts the thrashed straw into chaff, turns the stones for grinding the cattle-food into meal, and by a separate belt, when requisite, works a bone-crusher, in which, also, the hard American oilcake is broken down. Over the furnace is a drying-loft, where beans or damp corn are prepared for the better action of the millstones, by the waste heat of the engine fire. The strawchaff is carried to the root-house, where, by

Moody's machine, turnips, mangold, &c., may be described as ground down rather than cut, and the roots and chaff are then mixed together. . . . This mixture forms the staple winter food of the cattle and sheep, cake and corn being added in such proportions as are deemed necessary. The cut straw is not, even in this state, thought so soluble as it should be, and a large steaming-chest is being erected, in which the steam from the engine-boiler will be employed in preparing every substance used as food to afford its entire nutritive powers to the animal. The mess so prepared will consist of cut straw-chaff, ground roots, meal, oilcake or bran, and crushed furze; for Mr. Huxtable turns nature to account in all her productions, and the scrubby furze, which is, except in Wales, generally looked on as a nuisance, is here enlisted into the service of adding to the nation's food. After due inquiry, he satisfied himself that, properly used, this is a most nutritious substance. It becomes, therefore, an object of careful cultivation, and when crushed and steamed in conjunction with other materials, adds a flavour to the whole which, besides its nutritive qualities, makes an extremely palatable mess for any animal to which it is given. . . . Such is the winter food of the cattle and sheep.

Pigs are treated differently. They are kept as a manure factory, from which a given expenditure in meal will be returned, with the cost of attendance, in the increased value of the animals, and all the manure they leave be clear gain. . . . The pig food is therefore all purchased exclusively on their account, partly in the market, and partly from the inferior corn of the farm. . . .

The average stock of cattle kept is thirty milch cows and their calves, the whole of which are constantly housed, the younger being promoted from stall to stall as their elders depart under the butcher's charge. From 90 to 100 head are thus regularly kept on the farm. The cattle are all tied up in stalls, occupying three parallel rows, have plenty of light and air, and exhibit, notwithstanding constant confinement, the greatest liveliness and contentment. To econo-

Shaftesbury

Milton Abbas

mise as much as possible every particle of straw, they are all placed on sparred boards raised six inches above the water-tight floor; by this arrangement the straw is kept dry, and fully half the usual supply of litter is saved. The liquid is collected in an underground drain, whence it passes off to the tank. The cattle-house is very cheaply constructed, the walls being of wattled furze, which admits air without producing a draught, and the roof is thatched with straw, as being not only more economical in first cost, but far better adapted than a slate or tile roof to insure an equable temperature, being warm in winter and cool in summer. . . .

A little way further down is the establishment for the collection and preparation of manure. It comprises two extensive water-tight tanks for liquid, and a house in two compartments for the different kinds of solid manure. Here every element that is not carried off in the substance of the cattle, the sheep and the pigs, is carefully preserved, to be again in due time restored to the soil, and the slender stream which constantly runs into the liquid manure tank is directed into a box filled with gypsum, through which it is passed, in order to fix the ammonia, described by Mr. Huxtable as 'the spirit-like essence of the farm, ever longing and struggling to fly off into the boundless air.' It would occupy too much space to detail all the other processes going on on this farm, the dissolving of bones, the extraction of ammonia from rags, the conversion of earth by fire into an absorbent of liquid manure, – all these must be examined to be thoroughly appreciated.

Mention of steam power serves to remind us that we have reached the era of railways. By the end of the nineteenth century even the remotest Wessex hamlet was within a few miles of a railway station, and many had their own halt. The consequences were profound for everyone, not the least being the impact on the tourist trade. A rash of guidebooks appeared, extolling the virtues of the countryside, and pandering to the Victorian obsession with the minutiae of church architecture. For purpleness of prose it *would be hard to beat these offerings from the 1875 edition of a guide to Dorsetshire published by Adam and Charles Black.*

Milton Abbas

A pleasant and leafy lane winds up a gentle slope to one of the prettiest of Dorsetshire villages. It was built by the first Earl of Dorchester, and consists of two rows of the neatest cottages imaginable, with thatched roofs and quaint lattices, lining each side of a well-kept road. In the distance rises a range of verdurous hills. Each cottage stands in an open plot of ground, where the leafy chestnut rears its thick branches, and flings its far-spreading shadow, and where many a favourite English flower delights the senses with its charming bloom and honest hearty fragrance. The neat village inn is situated at the end of 'the street'; the almshouse and the fine old church stand in the centre opposite one another. No artist will omit to perpetuate in his sketch-book his visit to Milton Abbas.

On leaving the village we immediately descend into the deep shady hollow where Milton Abbey retires from the work-day world. Its park spreads up the hills on either side, but the house itself is situated in the vale – as calm and tranquil a spot as poet or philosopher could desire. Easily enough may the imagination re-people these silent shades with cowled monks winding through the trees in processional pomp, or sitting apart upon the crisp green sward, and musing – it may be – upon passions only half-subdued, upon crushed hopes, upon a weary manhood, upon the atonement rendered by a life of solitude and sacrifice, upon all they feared, and all they durst anticipate. . . .

Between Cerne Abbas and Dorchester there is nothing to detain the tourist, though from the hills occasional views are obtained of the fair woodlands and lowlands beneath, which, if seen in the rich rosy light of a setting sun, assume a wondrous aspect of tender beauty. How great an influence upon the character of a landscape is exercised by *colour!* See the vale or the meadow in the pearly haze of morning, in the golden clearness of the noon, in the purple of the increasing twilight, and note how different an aspect it assumes, how different an impression it produces upon the heart! And it is just these things which the pilgrim a-foot should take especial note of; not only will their observation beguile the way and lessen the distance, but assist in storing the mind with the most precious knowledge, and in charming the fancy with an unfailing succession of new and delightful images.

Some of the visitors, too, were quite adept with a pen. Richard Le Gallienne (1866–1947) moved in the same literary and artistic circles as Oscar Wilde, Aubrey Beardsley and W.B. Yeats, and was a contributor to the notorious Yellow Book. *After the 'naughty nineties' he vanished into obscurity, but not before he had bicycled around the countryside gathering material for* TRAVELS IN ENGLAND, *which was published in 1900. Like everyone else, he wanted to say something different about Stonehenge.*

And Stonehenge, I remembered, had given me an unforgettable thrill of mystery, though that stone writing upon the green page of Salisbury Plain was in a language I could not read. But the shape of the letters alone had fascinated me – and, indeed, it is not merely fanciful to say that at a distance Stonehenge is not unlike a Hebrew inscription written in stone.

In Amesbury he could find no one to tell him the way to Pewsey, but then he discovered a signpost pointing to it at the edge of the village. Of Pewsey itself he is dismissive to the point of rudeness.

Pewsey is one of those places in which one is interested solely on account of some other place beyond them.

Le Gallienne goes on to compare Pewsey station, rather

implausibly, with Clapham Junction and Crewe. But what really fascinated him were the local customs.

The trees are particularly fine as you near a little village just on the border of the Stonehenge plain, called Lake. . . . Just past Lake House, you turn sharply to the left down a lane which begins with a cluster of farm buildings. On the door of one of the barns or stables you will notice the mouldering heads and feet of various small criminals – foxes, stoats and moles. So the head of a traitor once grinned at you from Temple Bar.

A big, black-bearded countryman, whose kind eyes relieved the sternness of his grim beard, was busy with some hay in one of the sheds, and a young man, his son, as it presently transpired, was putting his whole soul into the cleaning of some harness, which pleasantly jingled as he rubbed, purring to himself the while, after the manner of men who rub down horses. . . . Well, black-beard and his son looked up as I entered the lane, and I thought I would take the opportunity of satisfying an old curiosity about those poor mouldering heads and feet on the barn-door. No doubt anthropologists would tell us that they represent the relic of ancient sacrifices to dark earth deities, or perhaps were once offerings of ingratiation to the gods who preside over barns and stables, – the gods who keep the rats from the corn, and watch over the new-born foal. These theories I did not mention to my two friends, though I did hazard one which I have often heard, that those small offenders were thus gibbeted for the same reason that highwaymen once dangled in chains at the cross-roads, – *pour encourager les autres.* This theory raised a smile, as at an outworn superstition, upon the faces of my countryman and his son. Yet the son was inclined to believe, he said, that if you tarred a rat and let it run loose among its friends and relations, it created an excellent effect. But, that apart, he would explain my sacrifice to dark earth deities on more immediately practical grounds. These animals were thus nailed up, not in the least as

Biddestone

tradesmen nail bad half-crowns to their counters, or for any such monitory or symbolic reason, but entirely for the purpose of simple enumeration. As once in an earlier England a price was set upon the heads of wolves, so in present-day England a price is set upon the tails of rats. You come to the farmer and say, 'I have slain so many rats, or so many stoats'; and the farmer says, 'Where are they?' Then you proudly take him to the barn-door and point to your victims neatly nailed in rows, and making something of a grisly decorative scheme. Then the farmer pays.

Weasels and stoats bring twopence a piece, rats 'a penny a tail' if caught up in the fields, and twopence if caught in 'a gin' down in the valley, near the stacks and barns. . . . Moles likewise bring a penny a tail, and then, in their case, there are the coats to think of, to avoid spoiling which special mole-traps are used. All this I felt was really valuable information, and I learnt, too, that the difference between a stoat and a weasel lay in a white spot upon the stoat's tail. In another county I have found that sparrows' eggs are a similar lucrative source of income. One farmer of my acquaintance gives a penny a dozen for them, and has paid over a pound this year to village boys for such blood-money – which means something like three thousand sparrows less in the world.

Another custom which would surely have intrigued Le Gallienne was a tendency on the part of the aristocracy to make fools of themselves in winter by sliding about on frozen ponds. Once again we are indebted to the keen observations of a participating clergyman, who noted the following in his diary.

Tuesday, 27 December 1870

After dinner drove into Chippenham with Perch and bought a pair of skates at Benk's for 17/6. Back to Langley and picked up Pelly. Drove to Draycot and she brought the carriage back. Across the fields to the Draycot water

and the young Awdry ladies chaffed me about my new skates. I had not been on skates since I was here last, 5 years ago, and was very awkward for the first ten minutes, but the knack soon came again. There was a distinguished company on the ice, Lady Dangan, Lord and Lady Royston and Lord George Paget all skating. Also Lord and Lady Sydney and a Mr. Calcraft. . . . I had the honour of being knocked down by Lord Royston, who was coming round suddenly on the outside edge. A large fire of logs burning within an enclosure of wattled hurdles. Harriet Awdry skated beautifully and jumped over a half sunken punt. Arthur Law skating jumped over a chair on its legs. The ice in splendid order and the sliders kept at the lower end of the water and divided from the skaters by a rope lying on the ice.

Sunday, New Year's Day, 1871

. . . When Perch came back from skating at Draycot last night, he amused us with an account of Friday's and Saturday's doings on the ice. On Friday they had a quadrille band from Malmesbury, skated quadrilles, Lancers, and Sir Roger de Coverley. Then they skated up and down with torches, ladies and gentlemen pairing off and skating arm in arm, each with a torch. There were numbers of Chinese lanterns all round the water, blue, crimson and green lights, magnesium riband, and a fire balloon was sent up. . . . While people were standing about in groups or skating up and down gently young Spencer skated up suddenly with outstretched arm to shake hands with Teddy. At the critical moment his skate hitched and he lost his balance and made a deep but involuntary obeisance before Perch, describing 'an attenuated arch', with his fingers and toes resting on the ice. People hid their faces, turned and skated away with a sour smile or grinning with repressed laughter. Perch stood still waiting for the 'attenuated arch' to unbind itself and retrieve its erect posture, 'looking on with a face like a

The bridge, Bradford on Avon

Sandy Lane

stone'. Gradually the 'arch' rose from its deep obeisance. The arch was the arch described by an attenuated tom cat. During the torch skating Harriet Awdry hurled her half-burnt torch ashore. Lord Cowley was walking up and down the path on the bank watching with great impatience the skaters whom he detests. The fiery torch came whirling and flaming through the dark and hit the noble diplomatist sharply across the shins, rebounding from which it lay blazing at the foot of a tree. Lord Cowley was very angry. 'I wish these people wouldn't throw their torches about here at me,' grumbled his lordship. 'Come away and hide behind the island or he'll see you,' said Perch to Harriet. So they glided away and from the cover of the island they watched Lord Cowley angrily beating the blazing torch against the ground to try to put it out. But the more he beat it, the more the torch flamed and showered sparks into his face. . . .

The skating clergyman was Francis Kilvert, whose diaries, when discovered and published in an abridged form between 1938 and 1940, were immediately recognized as classics of their genre, and have attracted a devoted following ever since. Kilvert is generally associated with the Welsh borderland around Hay-on-Wye and Clyro, but in fact a considerable portion of his diaries relate to the Chippenham area, especially Hardenhuish, where he was born in 1840, and Langley Burrell, where he served as his father's curate from 1872 to 1876. The following entry is a fine example of the diaries' style and illustrates well the character of the man who wrote them. It records a day spent visiting old friends during a New Year holiday at Langley Burrell.

Wednesday, 10 January, 1872

This morning at prayers the pretty housemaid Elizabeth with the beautiful large soft eyes was reading aloud in Luke i how Zacharias saw a vision in the Temple, but for the word 'vision' she substituted 'venison'.

After dinner I went to see old Jacob Smith who used to be head carter at Sheldon when I lived at Lanhill. He lives with his son-in-law and daughter Joseph and Mary Hatherell in one of the new cottages in St. Paul's district [Chippenham] at the top of Greenway Lane. The old man had a fall the other day and I found him upstairs in his bedroom, but sitting up in an easy chair. He looked very much the same as he used to when following his plough and his two famous bay and black horses, Diamond and Flower, though he is 77 years old. He said he knew me directly by my voice. We talked over the old times and the old people and we had many ancient memories in common. I asked after the old labourers on the farms. And some of them were dead long since and some were gone away. Isaac Parsons and Isaac Barton the Sheldon cattle men, they were dead. The latter had gone mad and died in the Lunatic Asylum. And Farmer John Blake of Biddestone, he was dead, and his brother Joseph the butcher had taken a farm at Hartham. Henry Stevens had moved to Yatton Keynell and was working for Farmer Taylor, and Ed'ard Bishop, the one-eyed man, he is now head man on Lanhill Farm, and old James Alexander he is crippled by rheumatism and crawls down to the house from Wellclose every day for a bit to do odd jobs about the place, and his daughter Ellen who was housemaid at the Farm she married a man named Banks and lives at Tytherton below Wick Hill, and Edward Fry, the one-armed bailiff, and Anne his wife and their three children they live at the new cottages by Lanhill Farm. Anne used to be cook at the farm. She was always a jolly good-humoured girl. I always liked her. I remember so well how she and Edward always came to Harnish Church on fine Sunday afternoons when they were courting. And old William Hulbert of Biddestone who always wore a crimson plush waistcoat, the large hale hearty man with the iron grey hair and the venerable handsome face, he is now the oldest man in Biddestone, the patriarch of the village. And John Spackman the shepherd who lived at Starveall he is gone away.

And then there was Thomas Swindon, the slouching rheumatic carter who walked so heavy and tender upon his feet, and Ammon Billet, who went with the oxen and was the wit of the farm, and Lewin Alexander who drove the oxen for his plough. I can see those oxen now. Old roan grey Flower with the long horns and the fore ox, and Pretty, red and white and short horn, and Blossom, a short-horned strawberry grey, and Broad, a Hereford ox, and I can still seem to hear Ammon and Lewin calling to the oxen, addressing them as 'old men' and 'boys' and cheering them on.

Then I walked on to Kington St. Michael. On the way I called at the Hulls' in Hardenhuish. Old Francis was at home, and Mrs. Hull, and a showy handsome girl with earrings whom I found to be Emma, and a tall handsome fair-haired soldier from the West Indies, Bermuda, with a fair heavy moustache, who was Alfred, and whom I remember to have seen last as an innocent chuckle-headed school boy with a shock of light hair and a round smock frock or pinafore. We talked of all the absent ones. Patty married to the butler of the family she lived with, and Bessie married and living in the 'shrub' (shrubbery), the 'wilderness' near Hardenhuish House. Maurice working at Woolwich Arsenal and helping to cast the last and greatest gun.

Jim married and living in the 'new' cottages now 20 years old, close by, Fanny in service at Melksham, and doing well, and 'Tommy Titymouse' out in the world, a grown man at work. How familiar all the dear old names. Old Francis spoke sadly about the changes in the parish, no school, the singing fallen, things so different from what they were.

As I left the cottage and went on to Kington the white frost of the morning had changed to rain and the weather had become warm. I went up to the top of the village to see my old friend Master Joseph Duckett. He did not recollect me till I told him my name. Then he was all animation. 'How are you, Master Duckett?' 'Through mercy,' said the old man with an earnest look from his keen glittering eyes, 'through mercy,' he repeated, 'I am well. I have been holden up wonderful. I have been made a wonder to myself.'

When we parted 'God bless you,' he said, 'and your labours.' An uncommon man. A broad massive earnest kindly face, and keen piercing eyes under shaggy grey penthouse brows, a venerable head of grey hair, a real crown of glory, and something undefinable about the man which marks his good blood.

As I came down the village I hunted up Mrs. Willis the old cook at Langley Rectory. She has been sorely tried by having three dumb children more or less idiots, one happily died and another happily likely to die.

The eldest child a noble stout girl of ten, dumb and silly, sat by the fire laughing strangely and making idle noises. She began to play with me. Her mother said the child was very fond of music and caught up tunes with an exceedingly quick ear.

At the vicarage I found Delmé and Graham Awdry spending part of their Sydney College holidays.

Edward Awdry said that an old man named Tarrant was still living in the Kington almshouses, who had waited on old Ayliffe White at Kington House. He was with him when he died and heard his last words. He was dressing his master and had raised him up in his arms when the old man dropped his head to one side and said, 'Willum, what d'ye think on't?'

Among Kilvert's interests was poetry, and from the occasional throwaway line in his diary we gather that he not only read, but also wrote, poems. Not surprisingly, in view of his insatiable curiosity about country people and their lives, he was particularly attracted by the work of the contemporary rural poets, and of one man in particular. The elderly William Barnes was a Dorset man who had distinguished himself locally as a schoolmaster, scholar, and for the last twenty-six years of his long life as a clergyman; but he also achieved a national reputation for his

Maiden Castle

sensitive (and sometimes sentimental) poetry in the Dorset dialect. It is his statue, not Hardy's, which adorns the centre of Dorchester. All his poetry is rooted in the people and landscape of the county he loved.

The primrwose in the sheade do blow,
The cowslip in the zun,
The thyme upon the down do grow,
The clote where streams do run;
An' where do pretty maidens grow
An' blow, but where the tów'r
Do rise among the bricken tuns,
In Blackmwore by the Stour?

If you could zee their comely gait,
An' pretty feaces' smiles,
A-trippen on so light o' waight,
An' steppen off the stiles;
A-gwain to church, as bells do swing
An' ring within the tow'r,
You'd own the pretty maidens' pleace
Is Blackmwore by the Stour.

If you vrom Wimborne took your road,
To Stower or Paladore,
An' all the farmers' housen show'd
Their daeters at the door;
You'd cry to bachelors at hwome –
'Here, come: 'ithin an hour
You'll vind ten maidens to your mind,
In Blackmwore by the Stour.'

An' if you looked 'ithin their door,
To zee em in their pleace,
A-doen housework up avore
Their smilen mother's feace;
You'd cry – 'Why, if a man would wive
An' thrive, 'ithout a dow'r,
Then let en look en out a wife
In Blackmwore by the Stour.'

As I upon my road did pass
A school-house back in May
There out upon the beaten grass
Wer maidens at their play;
An' as the pretty souls did twile
An' smile, I cried, 'The flow'r
O' beauty, then, is still in bud
In Blackmwore by the Stour.'

Kilvert's admiration for the poetry of William Barnes prompted him to write to the master, and his diary makes no secret of his joy when invited to pay a visit to Dorchester to meet him.

Thursday, May Eve 1874

This will always be a happy and memorable day in my remembrance.

Today I visited and made the acquaintance and I hope the friendship of William Barnes, the great idyllic Poet of England. Up at 6 o'clock, breakfast at 6.30, and left Chippenham by the 7.15 train. It was a glorious morning, fresh and exhilarating, as I started on my journey and the unclouded sky shone with a splendid blue over the brilliant green elms and the rich warm golden brown of the oaks.

The elms performed a solemn dance circling round each of the fine Church Towers of Somerset as we sped down into Dorset by the windings of the Frome and the elms of Castle Cary. And then the high downs began to rise and we seemed to breathe the sweet salt air as soon as we saw the bold white chalk cliffs that look to the blue sea.

Mr. Henry Moule, the Vicar of Fordington for nearly half a century, met me at the Dorchester Station, pointed out to me the great Roman amphitheatre, Maiden Castle, the vallum of the Roman camp, and took me round the beautiful avenues of luxuriant sycamore and chestnut which surround and adorn the town with delightful boulevards foursquare and exquisite shaded walks overarched by trees which give the place the look of a foreign town.

Gold Hill, Shaftesbury

Winterbourne Dauntsey

As we passed along the beautiful water walk and over the hatches between the crystal streams of the Frome and the bright watermeadows below and looked up at the picturesque old high town bosomed in its groves of sycamore and chestnut and tufted with lofty trees we met a lovely girl dressed in deep mourning and walking with her lover, probably a bold handsome artilleryman from the barracks, splendid in blue and gold. . . .

We walked together to the Poet's house, Winterbourne Came Rectory, about a mile from Fordington. The house lies a little back from the glaring white high road and stands on a lawn fringed with trees. It is thatched and a thatched verandah runs along its front. The thatched roof gives the Rectory house the appearance of a large lofty cottage. As we turned in at the iron gates from the high road and went down the gravel path the poet was walking in the verandah. He welcomed us cordially and brought us into his drawing room on the right-hand side of the door. He is an old man, over seventy, rather bowed with age, but apparently hale and strong. 'Excuse my study gown,' he said. He wore a dark grey loose gown girt round the waist with a black cord and tassel, black knee breeches, black silk stockings and gold buckled shoes.

I was immediately struck by the beauty and grandeur of his head. It was an Apostolic head, bald and venerable, and the long soft silvery hair flowed on his shoulders and a long white beard fell upon his breast. His face was handsome and striking, keen yet benevolent, the finely pencilled eyebrows still dark and a beautiful benevolent loving look lighted up his fine dark blue eyes when they rested upon you. He is a very remarkable and a very remarkable-looking man, half hermit, half enchanter.

The Poet seemed pleased with my visit and gratified that I had come such a long way to see him. I told him I had for many years known him through his writings and had long wished to thank him in person for the many happy hours his poems had given me. He smiled and said he was very glad if he had given me any pleasure. Frequently stroking his face and his venerable white beard the Poet told me he had composed his poems chiefly in the evening as a relaxation from the day's work when he kept a school in Dorchester. . . .

At the earnest request of the Vicar the Poet read aloud to us his admirable poem describing how worthy Bloom the Miller went to London to see the great 'glassen house' and how he could not get into the omnibus by reason of his bulk though he declared he was a poor starved Dorset man. We were all three in roars of laughter.

Then to please me he read his beautiful poem called 'Happiness'. It is one of my favourites. He said that 'No So's' means 'No Souls', i.e. friends, neighbours. 'No So's.' 'No my friends.' He read in a low voice, rather indistinct and with much feeling. 'I like your pathetic pieces best,' said the Vicar. 'So do I,' said the Poet. . . .

They had been accustomed there at some place in the neighbourhood to pass the cup to each other with a nod of the head. At one church there were two male communicants. When the cup was given to the first he touched his forelock and said, 'Here's your good health, Sir'. The other said, 'Here's the good health of our Lord Jesus Christ'.

One day there was christening and no water in the Font. 'Water, Sir!' said the clerk in astonishment. 'The last parson never used no water. He spit into his hand.'

We shall leave Kilvert enjoying, not for the first time, an anecdote he heard from a parishioner.

Monday, 16 December 1872

. . . Mrs. Banks told again the story of old Dame Matthews and the man who stole the pound of butter which her mother old Mrs. Thomas Knight used to be so fond of telling.

Dame Matthews used to live at the Home Farm at Langley Burrell. She was a member of the family, but she must have lived a long time ago, as Mrs. Banks remarked, because she called cows 'kine'. The Dame used to sit in the chimney corner and near her chair there was a little window through which she could see all down the dairy. One evening she saw one of the farm men steal a pound of butter out of the dairy and put it into his hat, at the same moment clapping his hat upon his head.

'John,' called the Dame. 'John, come here. I want to speak to you.' John came, carefully keeping his hat on his head. The Dame ordered some ale to be heated for him and bade him sit down in front of the roaring fire. John thanked his mistress and said he would have the ale another time, as he wanted to go home at once.

'No, John. Sit you down by the fire and drink some hot ale. 'Tis a cold night and I want to speak to you about the kine.'

Then the Vicar of Fordington told us of the state of things in his parish when he first came to it nearly half a century ago. No man had ever been known to receive the Holy Communion except the parson, the clerk and the sexton. There were 16 women communicants and most of them went away when he refused to pay them for coming.

Declaring the poll, Swindon, 1910

Oare

The miserable John, daring neither to take off his hat nor go without his mistress's leave sat before the scorching fire drinking his hot ale till the melting butter in his hat began to run down all over his face. The Dame eyed him with malicious fun. 'Now, John,' she said, 'you may go. I won't charge you anything for the butter.'

Nine months later, on 16 September 1873, we find Kilvert and his family busily preparing for a family wedding which he was to conduct at Langley Burrell the next day. Meanwhile, twenty miles away in Swindon Town Hall, a young reporter on a local newspaper stood up to address the annual meeting of the Wiltshire Archaeological and Natural History Society on the history and antiquities of Swindon – a subject (and one imagines, an audience) with which he did not feel entirely comfortable. The

reputation of Richard Jefferies, novelist, nature-essayist and 'man of the fields', has undergone a revival during the last decade, so that now much of his prolific output – all crammed into about fifteen years of a short life – is once again available in print. His spiritual home was the Marlborough Downs, beneath which he was born in 1848; and it was tramping these chalk hills, and dreaming away summer days, that he found his inspiration.

There were grass-grown tumuli on the hills to which of old I used to walk, sit down at the foot of one of them, and think. Some warrior had been interred there in the ante-historic times. The sun of the summer morning shone on the dome of sward, and the air came softly up from the wheat below, the tips of the grasses swayed as it passed sighing faintly, it ceased, and the bees hummed by to the thyme and heathbells. I became absorbed in the glory of the day, the sunshine, the sweet air, the yellowing corn turning from its sappy green to summer's noon of gold, the lark's song like a waterfall in the sky. I felt at that moment that I was like the spirit of the man whose body was interred in the tumulus; I could only understand and feel his existence the same as my own. He was as real to me two thousand years after interment as those I had seen in the body. The abstract personality of the dead seemed as existent as thought. As my thought could slip back the twenty centuries in a moment to the forest-days when he hurled the spear, or shot with the bow, hunting the deer, and could return again as swiftly to this moment, so his spirit could endure from then till now, and the time was nothing. . . .

Resting by the tumulus, the spirit of the man who had been interred there was to me really alive, and very close. This was quite natural, as natural and simple as the grass waving in the wind, the bees humming, and the larks' songs. Only by the strongest effort of the mind could I understand the idea of extinction; that was supernatural, requiring a miracle; the immortality of the soul natural, like earth. Listening to the sighing of the grass I felt immortality as I felt the beauty of the summer morning, and I thought beyond immortality, of other conditions, more beautiful than existence, higher than immortality.

That there is no knowing, in the sense of written reasons, whether the soul lives on or not, I am fully aware. I do not hope or fear. At least while I am living I have enjoyed the idea of immortality, and the idea of my own soul. If then, after death, I am resolved without exception into earth, air, and water, and the spirit goes out like a flame, still I shall have had the glory of that thought. . . .

Sweetly the summer air came up to the tumulus, the grass sighed softly, the butterflies went by, sometimes alighting on the green dome. Two thousand years! Summer after summer the blue butterflies had visited the mound, the thyme had flowered, the wind sighed in the grass. The azure morning had spread its arms over the low tomb; and full glowing noon burned on it; the purple of sunset rosied the sward. Stars, ruddy in the vapour of the southern horizon, beamed at midnight through the mystic summer night, which is dusky and yet full of light. White mists swept up and hid it; dews rested on the turf; tender harebells drooped; the wings of the finches fanned the air – finches whose colours faded from the wings how many centuries ago! Brown autumn dwelt in the woods beneath; the rime of winter whitened the beech clump on the ridge; again the buds came on the wind-blown hawthorn bushes, and in the evening the broad constellation of Orion covered the east. Two thousand times! Two thousand times the woods grew green, and ring-doves built their nests. Day and night for two thousand years – light and shadow sweeping over the mound – two thousand years of labour by day and slumber by night. Mystery gleaming in the stars, pouring down in the sunshine, speaking in the night, the wonder of the sun and of far space, for twenty centuries round about this low and green-grown dome. Yet all that mystery and wonder is as nothing to the Thought that lies therein, to the spirit that I feel so close.

Realising that spirit, recognising my own inner consciousness, the psyche, so clearly, I cannot understand time. It is eternity now. I am in the midst of it. It is about me in the sunshine; I am in it, as the butterfly floats in the light-laden air. Nothing has to come; it is now. Now is eternity; now is the immortal life. Here this moment, by this tumulus, on earth, now; I exist in it. The years, the centuries, the cycles are absolutely nothing; it is only a moment since this tumulus was raised; in a thousand years more it will still be only a moment. To the soul there is no past and no future; all is and will be ever, in now. For artificial purposes time is mutually agreed on, but there is really no such thing. The shadow goes on upon the dial, the index moves round upon the clock, and what is the difference? None whatever. If the clock had never been set going, what would have been the difference? There may be time for the clock, the clock may make time for itself: there is none for me. . . .

How many words it has taken to describe so briefly the feelings and the thoughts that came to me by the tumulus; thoughts that swept past and were gone, and were succeeded by others while yet the shadow of the mound had not moved from one thyme-flower to another, not the breadth of a grass-blade. Softly breathed the sweet south wind, gently the yellow corn waved beneath; the ancient, ancient sun shone on the fresh grass and the flower, my heart opened wide as the broad, broad earth. I spread my arms out, laying them on the sward, seizing the grass, to take the fulness of the days. Could I have my own way after death I would be burned on a pyre of pine-wood, open to the air, and placed on the summit of the hills. Then let my ashes be scattered abroad – not collected in an urn – freely sown wide and broadcast. That is the natural interment of man – of man whose Thought at least has been among the immortals; interment in the elements. Burial is not enough, it does not give sufficient solution into the elements speedily; a furnace is confined. The high open air of the topmost hill, there let the tawny flame lick up the fragment called the body; there cast the ashes into the space it longed for while living. . . .

The silky grass sighs as the wind comes carrying the blue butterfly more rapidly than his wings. A large humble-bee burrs round the green dome against which I rest; my hands are scented with thyme.

Jefferies had a vivid eye for detail. Here, for example, he takes us inside Wick Farm, 'an ancient rambling building, the present form of which is the result of successive additions at different dates, and in various styles'. Such a building, he remarks, exists by itself on the edge of almost every village.

The house has somehow shaped and fitted itself to the character of the dwellers within it: hidden and retired among trees, fresh and green with cherry and pear against the wall, yet the brown thatch and the old bricks subdued in tone by the weather. This individuality extends to the furniture; it is a little stiff and angular, but solid, and there are nooks and corners – as the window-seat – suggestive of placid repose: a strange opposite mixture throughout of flowery peace and silence, with an almost total lack of modern conveniences and appliances of comfort – as though the sinewy vigour of the residents disdained artificial ease.

In the oaken cupboards – not black, but a deep tawny colour with age and frequent polishing – may be found a few pieces of old china, and on the table at tea-time, perhaps, other pieces, which a connoisseur would tremble to see in use, lest a clumsy arm should shatter their fragile antiquity. Though apparently so little valued, you shall not be able to buy these things for money – not so much because their artistic beauty is appreciated, but because of the instinctive clinging to everything old, characteristic of the place and people. These have been there of old time: they shall remain still. Somewhere in the cupboards, too, is a curiously carved piece of iron, to fit into the hand, with a front of steel before the fingers, like a skeleton rapier guard; it is the ancient steel with which, and a flint, the tinder and the sulphur match were ignited.

Up in the lumber-room are carved oaken bedsteads of unknown age; linen-presses of black oak with carved panels, and a drawer at the side for the lavender-bags; a rusty rapier, the point broken off; a flintlock pistol, the barrel of portentous length, and the butt weighted with a mace-like knob of metal, wherewith to knock the enemy on the head. An old yeomanry sabre lies about somewhere, which the good man of the time wore when he rode in the troop against the rioters in the days of machine-burning – which was like a civil war in the country, and is yet recollected and talked of. The present farmer, who is getting just a trifle heavy in the saddle himself, can tell you the names of labourers living in the village whose forefathers rose in that insurrection. It is a

Box Valley

memory of the house, how one of the family paid £40 for a substitute to serve in the wars against the French. . . .

The parlour is always full of flowers – the mantel-piece and grate in spring quite hidden by fresh green boughs of horse-chestnut in bloom, or with lilac, bluebells, or wild hyacinths; in summer nodding grasses from the meadows, roses, sweet-briar; in the autumn two or three great apples, the finest of the year, put as ornaments among the china, and the corners of the looking-glass decorated with bunches of ripe wheat. A badger's skin lies across the back of the armchair; a fox's head, the sharp white tusks showing, snarls over the doorway; and in glass cases are a couple of stuffed kingfishers, a polecat, a white blackbird, and a diver – rare here – shot in the mere hard by.

On the walls are a couple of old hunting pictures, dusky with age, but the crudity of the colours by no means toned down or their rude contrast moderated: bright scarlet coats, bright white horses, harsh green grass, prim dogs, stiff trees, human figures immovable in tight buckskins; running water hard as glass, the sky fixed, the ground all too small for the grouping, perspective painfully empha-sized, so as to be itself made visible; the surface every-where 'painty' – in brief, most of the possible faults compressed together, and proudly fathered by the artist's name in full.

No such criticism could be levelled at the verbal landscape painter of Wessex par excellence, Thomas Hardy. Here the master introduces us to Egdon Heath, the backcloth to his story of THE RETURN OF THE NATIVE, *published in 1878. The heath was identified by Hermann Lea, a contemporary commen-tator, as 'that vast expanse of moorland which stretches, prac-tically without a break, from Dorchester to Bournemouth'.*

A Saturday afternoon in November was approaching the time of twilight, and the vast tract of unenclosed wild known as Egdon Heath embrowned itself moment by moment. Overhead, the hollow stretch of whitish cloud shutting out the sky was as a tent which had the whole heath for its floor.

The heaven being spread with this pallid screen and the earth with the darkest vegetation, their meeting-line at the horizon was clearly marked. In such contrast the heath wore the appearance of an instalment of night which had taken up its place before its astronomical hour was come: darkness had to a great extent arrived hereon, while day stood distinct in the sky. Looking upwards, a furze-cutter would have been inclined to continue work; looking down, he would have decided to finish his faggot and go home. The distant rims of the world and of the firmament seemed to be a division in time no less than a division in matter. The face of the heath by its mere complexion added half an hour to the evening; it could in like manner retard the dawn, sadden noon, anticipate the frowning of storms scarcely generated, and intensify the opacity of a moonless midnight to a cause of shaking and dread. . . .

To recline on a stump of thorn in the central valley of Egdon, between afternoon and night, as now, where the eye could reach nothing of the world outside the summits and shoulders of heathland which filled the whole circum-ference of its glance, and to know that everything around and underneath had been from prehistoric times as un-altered as the stars overhead, gave ballast to the mind adrift on change, and harassed by the irrepressible New. The great inviolate place had an ancient permanence which the sea cannot claim. Who can say of a particular sea that it is old? Distilled by the sun, kneaded by the moon, it is renewed in a year, in a day, or in an hour. The sea changed, the fields changed, the rivers, the villages, and the people changed, yet Egdon remained.

In this next extract, Hardy describes contrasting Dorset landscapes, as the tragedy of TESS OF THE D'URBERVILLES *unfolds.*

It is a vale whose acquaintance is best made by viewing

it from the summits of the hills that surround it – except perhaps during the droughts of summer. An unguided ramble into its recesses in bad weather is apt to engender dissatisfaction with its narrow, tortuous and miry ways.

This fertile and sheltered tract of country, in which the fields are never brown and the springs never dry, is bounded on the south by the bold chalk ridge that embraces the prominences of Hambledon Hill, Bulbarrow, Nettlecombe-Tout, Dogbury, High Stoy, and Bubb Down. The traveller from the coast, who, after plodding northward for a score of miles over calcareous downs and corn-lands, suddenly reaches the verge of one of these escarpments, is surprised and delighted to behold, extended like a map beneath him, a country differing absolutely from that which he has passed through. Behind him the hills are open, the sun blazes down upon fields so large as to give an unenclosed character to the landscape, the lanes are white, the hedges low and plashed, the atmosphere colourless. Here, in the valley, the world seems to be constructed upon a smaller and more delicate scale; the fields are mere paddocks, so reduced that from this height their hedgerows appear a network of dark green threads overspreading the paler green of the grass. The atmosphere beneath is languorous, and is so tinged with azure that what artists call the middle distance partakes also of that hue, while the horizon beyond is of the deepest ultramarine. Arable lands are few and limited; with but slight exceptions the prospect is a broad rich mass of grass and trees, mantling minor hills and dales within the major. Such is the Vale of Blackmoor. . . .

It [the Frome valley] was intrinsically different from the Vale of Little Dairies, Blackmoor Vale, which, save during her disastrous sojourn at Trantridge, she had exclusively known till now. The world was drawn to a larger pattern here. The enclosures numbered fifty acres instead of ten, the farmsteads were more extended, the groups of cattle formed tribes hereabout; there only families. These myriads of cows stretching under her eyes from the far east to the far west outnumbered any she had ever seen at one glance before. The green lea was speckled as thickly with them as a canvas by Van Alsloot or Sallaert with burghers. The ripe hue of the red and dun kine absorbed the evening sunlight, which the white-coated animals returned to the eye in rays almost dazzling, even at the distant elevation on which she stood.

The bird's-eye perspective before her was not so luxuriantly beautiful, perhaps, as that other one which she knew so well; yet it was more cheering. It lacked the intensely blue atmosphere of the rival vale, and its heavy soils and scents; the new air was clear, bracing, ethereal. The river itself, which nourished the grass and cows of these renowned dairies, flowed not like the streams in Blackmoor. Those were slow, silent, often turbid; flowing over beds of mud into which the incautious wader might sink and vanish unawares. The Froom waters were clear as the pure River of Life shown to the Evangelist, rapid as the shadow of a cloud, with pebbly shallows that prattled to the sky all day long. There the water-flower was the lily; the crowfoot here.

Either the change in the quality of the air from heavy to light, or the sense of being amid new scenes where there were no invidious eyes upon her, sent up her spirits wonderfully. Her hopes mingled with the sunshine in an ideal photosphere which surrounded her as she bounded along against the soft south wind. She heard a pleasant voice in every breeze, and in every bird's note seemed to lurk a joy.

As the drama draws to its inevitable conclusion we find the fugitives – Tess and Angel Clare – making their way north, from Dorset into Wiltshire.

To walk across country without much regard to roads was not new to Tess, and she showed her old agility in the performance. The intercepting city, ancient Melchester [Salisbury], they were obliged to pass through in order to take advantage of the town bridge for crossing a large river that obstructed them. It was about midnight when they went along the deserted streets, lighted fitfully by the few lamps, keeping off the pavement that it might not echo their footsteps. The graceful pile of cathedral architecture rose dimly on their left hand, but it was lost upon them now. Once out of the town they followed the turnpike-road, which after a few miles plunged across an open plain.

Though the sky was dense with cloud a diffused light from some fragment of a moon had hitherto helped them a little. But the moon had now sunk, the clouds seemed to settle almost on their heads, and the night grew as dark as a cave. However, they found their way along, keeping as much on the turf as possible that their tread might not resound, which it was easy to do, there being no hedge or fence of any kind. All round was open loneliness and black solitude, over which a stiff breeze blew.

They had proceeded thus gropingly two or three miles further when on a sudden Clare became conscious of some vast erection close in his front, rising sheer from the grass. They had almost struck themselves against it.

'What monstrous place is this?' said Angel.

'It hums,' said she. 'Hearken!'

He listened. The wind, playing upon the edifice, produced a booming tune, like the note of some gigantic one-stringed harp. No other sound came from it, and lifting his hand and advancing a step or two, Clare felt the vertical surface of the structure. It seemed to be of solid stone, without joint or moulding. Carrying his fingers onward he found that what he had come in contact with was a colossal rectangular pillar; by stretching out his left hand he could feel a similar one adjoining. At an indefinite height overhead something made the black sky blacker, which had the semblance of a vast architrave uniting the pillars horizontally. They carefully entered beneath and between; the surfaces echoed their soft rustle; but they seemed to be still out of doors. The place was roofless.

Tess drew her breath fearfully, and Angel, perplexed, said –

'What can it be?'

Feeling sideways they encountered another tower-like pillar, square and uncompromising as the first; beyond it another and another. The place was all doors and pillars, some connected above by continuous architraves.

'A very Temple of the Winds,' he said.

The next pillar was isolated; others composed a trilithon; others were prostrate, their flanks forming a causeway wide enough for a carriage; and it was soon obvious that they made up a forest of monoliths grouped upon the grassy expanse of the plain. The couple advanced further into this pavilion of the night till they stood in its midst.

Hardy chose Stonehenge to stage the denouement of his greatest tragedy; but the same theatre could also be the scene of comedy. The naturalist and traveller, W.H. Hudson, attended the summer solstice gathering in 1908.

At Stonehenge I found a good number of watchers, about a couple of hundred, already assembled, but more were coming in continually, and a mile or so of the road to Amesbury visible from 'The Stones' had at times the appearance of a ribbon of fire from the lamps of this continuous stream of coming cyclists. Altogether about five to six hundred persons gathered at 'The Stones', mostly young men on bicycles who came from all the Wiltshire towns within easy distance, from Salisbury to Bath. I had a few good minutes at the ancient temple when the sight of the rude upright stones looking black against the moonlit and star-sprinkled sky produced an expected feeling in me: but the mood could not last; the crowd was too big and noisy, and the noises they made too suggestive of a bank-holiday crowd at the Crystal Palace.

At three o'clock a ribbon of slate-grey cloud appeared above the eastern horizon, and broadened by degrees, and

Stonehenge

pretty soon made it evident that the sun would be hidden at its rising at a quarter to four. The crowd, however, was not down-hearted; it sang and shouted; and by-and-by, just outside the barbed-wire enclosure a rabbit was unearthed, and about three hundred young men with shrieks of excitement set about its capture. It was a lively scene, a general scrimmage, in which everyone was trying to capture an elusive football with ears and legs to it, which went darting and spinning about hither and thither among the multitudinous legs, until earth compassionately opened and swallowed poor distracted bunny up. It was but little better inside the enclosure, where the big fallen stones behind the altar-stone, in the middle, on which the first rays of the sun would fall, were taken possession of by a crowd of young men who sat and stood packed together like guillemots on a rock. These too, cheated by that rising cloud of the spectacle they had come so far to see, wanted to have a little fun, and began to be very obstreperous. By-and-by they found out an amusement very much to their taste.

Motor-cars were now arriving every minute, bringing important-looking persons who had timed their journeys so as to come upon the scene a little before 3.45, when the sun would show on the horizon; and whenever one of these big gentlemen appeared within the circle of stones, especially if he was big physically and grotesque-looking in his motorist get-up, he was greeted with a tremendous shout. In most cases he would start back and stand still, astonished at such an outburst, and then, concluding that the only way to save his dignity was to face the music, he would step hurriedly across the green space to hide himself behind the crowd.

The most amusing case was that of a very tall person adorned with an exceedingly long, bright red beard, who had on a Glengarry cap and a great shawl over his overcoat. The instant this unfortunate person stepped into this arena a general wild cry of 'Scotland for ever!' was raised, followed by such cheers and yells that the poor man actually staggered back as if he had received a blow, then seeing there was no other way out of it, he too rushed across the open space to lose himself among the others.

All this proved very entertaining, and I was glad to laugh with the crowd, thinking that after all we were taking a very mild revenge on our hated enemies, the tyrants of the roads.

More from Hudson shortly, but first we shall return to one of those stalwart reporters of Wessex life, the clergy wives. In 1904 there appeared a small book – now long-forgotten – purporting to be by one Deborah Primrose, entitled A MODERN BOEOTIA: PICTURES FROM LIFE IN A COUNTRY PARISH. Boeotia was a region of classical Greece which had a reputation for the stupidity of its inhabitants, and a modern parallel – with Essex – had been drawn in 1884. Here, however, the epithet was applied to a village referred to as 'Snorum End', actually Winterbourne Bassett near Avebury.

The author of the book was in fact a Mrs Ottley, whose husband, a noted theologian, was rector of Winterbourne Bassett from 1897 until 1903, when he was appointed Professor of Pastoral Theology at Oxford University. She continued her literary endeavours, writing for magazines and, in 1905, publishing another book under the same pseudonym. This time she chose an extraordinary subject for the Edwardian wife of an Oxford professor of theology – BEAUTY OF FIGURE: HOW TO ACQUIRE AND RETAIN IT BY MEANS OF EASY AND PRACTICAL HOME EXERCISES. Presumably this was how she had whiled away her lonely sojourn in the rectory at Winterbourne Bassett.

North and south, straight as a bee-line, runs the white treeless road, with brown fields fresh from the plough, or fields green with sprouting corn, skirting either side of it as far as one can see; – an endless, wind-swept, sun-baked, dusty road. The northern horizon is bounded by two or three thatched cottages, just discernible when the sun shines on them; in the south, remotely distant, the far-off hills rise blue against the sky. In the foreground, and separated from the point where one stands only by a narrow valley where the sheep-bells tinkle, is the straight wall of the Downs standing like a rampart between us and the other side. They have a characteristic dignity and largeness of atmosphere, these flat-roofed lonely hills. The wind blows keenly over them, their silence is broken only by the noisy flight of a startled bird, or by the swift pattering of some scared rabbit. They possess certain attributes of the mountains whereby they are invested with a peculiar beauty of their own – in their silence, their largeness, their untrodden solitudes. And sometimes, odd as it may seem, how wonderfully like the sea they are! This strikes one specially on a typical July day, when the great billowy white clouds ride across the blue sky, and the hollows in the Downs look as if they have been scooped out afresh by some gigantic hand. Then shadows flit over their surface, multiform and many-hued, while up them and over them march the majestic batallions of the clouds, now burying them in purple shadow, now leaving them bathed in living light. Strangely, wonderfully like the sea! – And at one's back are the bare open fields; and the brown thatch of the cottages and the grey tower of the church peep out from the hollow where the village lies.

There is no luxuriance of nature anywhere. A waterless, almost treeless landscape meets the eye on every side. As for man, in these regions he wastes not an inch. To him earth is *useful* earth or nothing, and nature brings him no inspiration nor haunting vision of beauty; she is his stern bread-giver. Hence one looks in vain for the neatly-clipped hedgerows of Kent, or even for the moss-covered stone walls of Wales. Great wide patches of unfenced land constitute our fields, yet they have a strange beauty of their own, as they lie russet gold under a September sun, or purple in the twilight after the plough has furrowed them, or vividly green against the blue sky, where the swedes have been planted. . . .

Here the 'crops' are the first and great consideration, and hence it is that apart from the scarcity of trees, all sensible birds who set any store by existence, fly far from us. There are no woods, and no water except a 'brook,' which holds the drainage of a farm-yard, to say nothing of pots and pans innumerable, and which the villagers boast is 'part o' the river Temses.' And indeed it evidently has a high opinion of its importance, since its presence permeates the place with an odour all its own. Wild flowers too grow sparsely, and since every inch of road or field speaks of man and his pursuits, one cannot wonder if nature in her most tender and caressing moods seeks a refuge elsewhere. . . .

The village itself boasts of one shop, tiny of size, and much patronised by the babies, where the good lady sells, at *enormous* profit to herself, currants which might readily be mistaken for bullets, bread of massive weight, and sweets which savour of soap and hair oil. I should like to make an inspection of her domain one day. I never saw such a motley collection in any single shop of its size: onions, cheese, spirits of nitre, tobacco, tinned beef, hair-brushes, gloves, prayer-books, infants' comforters, boots, oranges, bacon, candles, sardines, Owbridge's lung tonic, and half the pharmacopoeia, are thrown together in magnificent confusion. And yet the old lady herself knows just where to lay her hand upon everything, and woe betide the miserable urchin who ventures to pilfer an orange or a ball of string! Then there are the blacksmith, the carpenter, and the inn-keeper, – as far below the people of the shop as they are above the rest of the village. The publican inhabits a beautiful white gabled cottage, with thatched and mossy roof, which he turns into anything but the abode of peace it looks. It is often full of quarrelsome and noisy men and women, though one wouldn't think, to hear their loud-mouthed piety, that they ever set foot in the place.

'Just think of that there Missus Jones and what a wicked base mother 'er do make to 'er dear childern. I doan't like 'er, I doan't, but then, thank the Lard, I doan't drink, and 'er do.' But the publican would have a very different tale to tell, if he spoke truly. As for him, he perhaps naturally does his best to make his trade a success, and he carried his theory so practically into operation one New Year's Eve as to bring to the church at midnight a quantity of beer, and therewith so befuddled our bell-ringers that one at least was forced there and then to take his sleep on the belfry floor, and thus peacefully snored in the New Year.

The remnant of the village consists of the labourers and milkers on the three farms, with their families. Among these, there are many whose ancestors have been born and buried here for generations, and who have never gone further afield than, by the aid of the carrier's cart, to the nearest town. Then too there are the good-for-nothings, who unfortunately are many in number, and who tramp from place to place, working on a farm for a year at a time, running up a long bill at the village shop, which they neither attempt nor mean to pay, and then suddenly decamping no one knows where. . . .

It is a lonely and a strange life which we have to live. The very sound of wheels is a surprise to us, and a ring at the door bell is as startling as a thunderclap. Yet, if we have to forego much that most people enjoy, we gain much too. We are obliged to fall back on the primal facts of life, upon the power and sweetness of love. We learn to have simple wants, to be easily pleased, to expect Tuesday to be exactly like Monday, in its every uneventful detail, and not to mind if it is; to hope much from the charities and joys of home, and to find, with deep content, that they at least do not fail or disappoint.

In addition to acting as the village social worker a clergy wife was expected to take an active interest in the life of the school, as the following extract shows.

My visitations to the school wake in me perpetual amazement at finding the children so uniformly meek and lamb-like; for volcanic fires, I know, lie smouldering there, and it needs only a new face to turn this holy peace into an uproar.

In the school lies our hope and our torment, – our torment, because there is always something wrong with it; either the teacher is ill, or the monitor rebellious, or the children and their parents are uncontrollable, or an epidemic is in full swing without our knowledge.

Some evil destiny seems to pursue our teachers here, for they appear to have been, from time immemorial, painfully shaky in body, or in morals. Mysterious stories loom out of the past concerning one teacher, self-styled a 'single woman,' whose distressed family and husband followed and found her here, six weeks after her arrival; concerning a master who one morning did not put in an appearance at the school-hour, whereupon a general hubbub ensued, until one urchin, wiser than the rest, undertook a search, and found the 'instructor of youth and morals,' lying prone beside his own beer-barrel, peacefully asleep.

Since our advent, I know not why, the shakiness has been transferred to the *bodies* of our teachers. Such curious, outlandish diseases, too, befall them, suited to the place. The worst and most oddly afflicted perhaps, was a cataleptic, who would reach the middle of a sentence, and then stand in a dumb trance for half-an-hour, while the children occupied themselves in ways and works which history does not relate. At the end of that time, she would serenely and suddenly finish the sentence, without any consciousness beyond vague astonishment at the rapid flight of time.

And indeed, is it a wonder, with such material, and in such a backwater of existence, that our teachers should habitually be somewhat abnormal and uncanny? Education! it is like making bricks without straw or tea with cold water, in a place like this.

Once a year the diocesan inspector arrives to test their 'religious knowledge,' which he always pronounces to be 'excellent;' and their powers of repetition, which appear likewise to be as near perfection as human efforts can be. He does somehow manage to elicit more from them than

Trying to keep still

can be gleaned on an ordinary day. I think it must have something to do with Sunday frocks and clean pinafores, and the generally freshening effect of a washed face.

Some of them on such occasions are set to write, and it is quite comical to see the poor victims gazing wildly round the room, as if the Catechism were inscribed in mid-air, scratching their heads, shuffling their feet, biting their nails, and finally scribbling away for dear life just as time is up. Some of the boys were once told off to write the Lord's Prayer. On the slate of a boy of eleven, I afterwards found this as the total result, and by comparison, it was more or less an average, typical production:

'Giv us our passes as we for giv them our passes. Lad us not inter tempteation. The pory and the gorly for heaver. All men.'

He possibly knew the sense, and let the sounds take care of themselves, but a doubt, fostered by their endless parrot repetitions of apparently unintelligible collects and hymns, suggests the probability that he understood nothing whatever of that which he wrote. A few other small boys, who were seized with an irresistible desire to contemplate closely the quality of the slate-pencil belonging to their neighbours, were told to write a short life of John the Baptist. This was the result on one slate picked up haphazard:

'St John the Baby was a prest and is cloes made of kammer skin and he ad a leathern girgle about his weast and is mother Elizebeth and is father name John and food was lukes and wild honney from the rocks and a Angle came to John and said though shalt beer a son and is father would not believe it and he was dome till he beer the son and his tongue was loosed and he spake. And John catched a marackuas draft of fishes and Ponteous Pillipip killed im, and ad is ed brought in for supper on a dish.' . . .

We once had a teacher who gave up the minds of the children as incapable of improvement, and so set to work on their behaviour. On this subject she used to wax tearfully eloquent, warning the children that unless they reformed their ways, they would 'never grow up into little ladies and gentlemen!'

Immediately, a new rule was instituted; each girl on meeting me was to give a curtsey, each boy a salute, and we were all to exchange a civilised greeting and smile. For a time all went well. There was a reign of almost terrifying politeness. Whenever I entered school, there was a universal bobbing and saluting, and a scrimmage on the part of three or four boys to close the door after me. If I met the children in the street, there was a profuse interchange of compliments; indeed, so anxious were they to forget none of their duties, that I was often designated 'governess,' 'teacher,' or 'zurr.'

One day a small boy started a new rule on his own account, and gave a low and solemn curtsey to me as I passed. I knew by the suppressed giggles of an admiring group, that this meant rebellion. The schoolmistress, hearing by chance of the episode, was shocked beyond expression at such ungentlemanly behaviour, and the next stage in the affair consisted in the arrival of a batch of letters written by indignant schoolfellows who, acting under orders, had sent the poor little mortal to Coventry.

'I am asheamed,' wrote one in the fire of his indignation, 'that any boy in our skole should have moked up in your feace and laffed when you have been so good to us. Teacher is greaved, so is we all, and we are not going to speek to him nor play with him for a week, he shall do all alone.'

How I laughed over those letters, all of which bore marks of the 'aggreavement' of the teacher, and how I secretly pitied the small culprit as I saw him marching mournfully from school by himself! On the eighth day, when the period of Coventry was at an end, and he was being accompanied home by quite a crowd of 'greaved' and 'shocked' fellow-creatures, I chanced to meet him. All, including the offender, assumed their very best behaviour till I had passed, but happening to look after them, I saw him doing what any boy of spirit would have done under the circumstances. He was bobbing and curtseying as fast as his fat legs could manage it, and I saw all that 'greaved' crowd standing round, chuckling and shaking with 'laffter.' I took great precautions that this time the teacher should hear nothing of it, and she lived on, in the blissful delusion that her endeavours were crowned with success.

Another powerful influence in many villages, especially where the hold of the church was none too strong, was the village preacher. Richard Jefferies described one in terms which suggest a striking continuity from the world of the medieval pilgrim and saint, with which our book began.

Pausing once to listen to such a man, who was preaching in a roadside cottage in a loud and excited manner, I found he was describing, in graphic if rude language, the procession of a martyr of the Inquisition to the stake. His imagination naturally led him to picture the circumstances as corresponding to the landscape of fields with which he had been from youth familiar. The executioners were dragging the victim bound along a footpath across the meadows to the pile which had been prepared for burning him. When they arrived at the first stile they halted, and held an argument with the prisoner, promising him his life and safety if he would recant, but he held to the faith.

Then they set out again, beating and torturing the sufferer along the path, the crowd hissing and reviling. At the next stile a similar scene took place – promise of pardon, and scornful refusal to recant, followed by more torture. Again, at the third and last stile, the victim was finally interrogated, and, still firmly clinging to his belief, was committed to the flames in the centre of the field. Doubtless there was some historic basis for the story; but the preacher made it quite his own by the vigour and life of the local colouring in which he clothed it, speaking of the green grass, the flowers, the innocent sheep, the faggots, and so on, bringing it home to the minds of his audience to

whom faggots and grass and sheep were so well known. They worked themselves into a state of intense excitement as the narrative approached its climax, till a continuous moaning formed a deep undertone to the speaker's voice. Such men are not paid, trained, or organized; they labour from goodwill in the cause.

Alfred Williams, whose name is often linked with that of Jefferies, was a poet, folk-song collector, and shrewd observer of the country scene, as well as working as a hammerman in the Swindon railway works. In 1912 he published a composite portrait of the Wiltshire village, based on his experiences of the area around South Marston, where he lived. Here is an anecdote about the village chapel.

Just down the lane, a short way from the church, is a tiny dissenting chapel. It is no bigger than a poor man's dwelling, and is almost out of sight, hemmed in with apple-trees on one side and a quaint thatched cottage on the other. I have known the time when quite a crowd frequented the place, but it is almost deserted now. The percentage of worshippers in villages, as in towns, is on the wane; there is a tragic falling off in numbers at church and chapel, too. Pausing without the door the other evening, and chancing to peer inside, I saw there were but three occupants, the preacher, his wife, and one poor old woman beside, and she has died since.

But there have been rousing scenes in the chapel in times gone by. Then conversions were a common occurrence. There were mid-week services and open-air meetings. Pressing invitations were sent round to the poor folk, and a good attendance was the inevitable result. Preachers came from all the villages and towns in the neighbourhood; there was great and endless variety of sermons and doctrine. William Keen was the superintendent then. He was a stout champion of Nonconformity, and a stalwart progressive politician as well. His work lay in the manufactory at the railway town. All day or night he slaved in

Flamstone, near Bishopstone

Tilshead

the rolling-mills amongst the blazing white-hot iron, and walked to and from the village. This he did for nearly fifty years, and after that procured an old tricycle, as heavy as a wagon almost, and trundled that along. His hair and side-whiskers were grey, and his face very red; it was said he was fond of a glass, but what of that? His work was abnormally hot and exacting, and whatever he took, he earned it. I have no patience at all to listen to those who would damn a man for taking a glass of beer, whether he be Christian, Turk, or Infidel.

There was no music at all at the chapel in those days. William Keen started the singing, and the others joined in, young and old together; it was a very homely crowd at all times. Grandfather Bridges was there, and his wife Letitia, both very devout indeed. One old lady declared she felt so light she could jump over the housetop; and another worshipper's frequent and fervent expression was that they would sweep the enemy away 'with the beesom of destruction.' He also hoped the Almighty would amend the ways of the Anglicans, or otherwise 'bring them all pell-mell into a whip (heap) o' stwuns.'

I remember one old local preacher, named Maslin, who used to come to the chapel now and then, clad in a white smock reaching halfway below the knees. This old fellow was an agricultural labourer, and lived far away over the downs. He was very short in stature, with grey hair, and exceedingly bronzed and sunburnt; he had toiled among the sheep and lambs, the wheat and oats, and had heard the lark sing in the blue heavens thousands of times. He had also felt the cold nipping wind sweeping up the valley and over the hill-tops, and had trudged through the deep snow to the village over and over again. When he came to preach he carried his dinner tied up in a red handkerchief and hung on a blackthorn stick over his shoulder. His fare was very simple – bread and cheese, and he must have a glass of ale with it from somewhere or other; he did not indulge in hot cooked food that day. A great number used to go and hear him preach; he could always command a

congregation, he was so sternly simple, outspoken, and comical. He was a firm believer in the devil as a personality. Once when he had been called to see a sick man, and had not been able to make a very deep impression on the unfortunate, he attributed it all to the actual presence of the Evil One. 'I know'd 'a was ther,' the old man declared most gravely, 'for I could smell the brimstone; the house was full on't.'

But what I have to tell you is more seriously comical than all this, and it is gospel truth. One Sunday evening, in late autumn, he was down to preach, and there was the usual full attendance; the little chapel was packed; a great time was expected; they were not all disappointed. Old Maslin was beside himself, and preached vehemently. As the sermon proceeded – it was half sermon and half prayer – he waxed hotter and hotter. Now he leaned far forward over the rails of the pulpit, now jumped backward, stamped hard with his feet, and swayed from side to side. The congregation perspired, and trembled in their pews. Louder and louder the old fellow's voice pealed out; he stamped harder and harder; everyone felt something was to happen, and happen it did. There was a large iron stove in that chapel; it stood in the centre. The pipes from this went up and then passed horizontally to the wall some distance away. Moreover, they had not been swept out for a long time, and were become very foul. The storm raged with increasing fury. The old folk were getting uncomfortable; the young girls tittered. The preacher shouted at the top of his voice, and stamped mightily with his feet. 'Send the power, and send it now!' he cried. One more moment, and it came. The joints of the pipes could stand no longer. With a shuddering crack the whole lot of the horizontals toppled down. A loud yell went up from the people; the youth exploded; but there were no heads broken. There was a prompt young man sitting just underneath that pipe. At the first crack he leapt up and caught it falling; but he made a sinister use of the opportunity. Receiving the pipes in the middle, with a dexterous

Abbotsbury

The River Stour, near Sturminster

movement of the hands, he twirled them round, and shot vast clouds of soot over all the people from one end of the place to the other. The result may be better imagined than described; it was like a pandemonium. All Maslin's preaching faded beside that night; that was his veritable *coup d'éclat*.

The works of Jefferies and Williams were written for a sophisticated audience – those who in late Victorian and Edwardian England found themselves living in huge cities while retaining a nostalgia for the country parishes from which their parents or grandparents had escaped. The novels of Thomas Hardy provided a similar appeal, and the region with which we are concerned was already being dubbed the 'Hardy Country'. But how was the Hardy Country changing? So asked a journalist of an old Dorset shepherd, who in 1910 was living in Dorchester workhouse, aged 100. The response was not what he was expecting.

'And which is Mr Green?' I asked.

'Here he is,' promptly replied one of the ancients, turning and slapping the centenarian on the shoulder with an air of amusement and pride combined, indicating what was shown again and again later, that the centenarian was a great favourite, and the chief *raconteur* and humourist of the company. 'Here he is – Job Green, but they generally calls him "Jobey," don't they, Jobey, eh?'

'Eh, what d'ye say?' queried the man of three figures, putting his hand to his ear in the form of a speaking trumpet. . . .

'You don't mind what they do call 'ee – so long's they don't call 'ee too late for breakfast, eh?' interjected a professor at this breakfast table of the wits.

'Not I,' answered Jobey, sturdily.

'Where were you born, Job?' asked I, beginning in the approved chronological method – at the beginning.

'I wer barn,' replied the centenarian, throwing himself into a reminiscent mood, 'up into a leane up above Toller Poorhousen' (the ancient man invariably uses the Saxon plural ending 'en' in words like house and place). 'It's a deairy house down there now, on the Kingcombe Road. La, I do mind when there was only a grove o' mud-walled housen there! I lived in a house that father put up – they used to put 'em up in them there days – a bit of a voundation, an' all the hrest o' it mud-walls, a hroofed wi' thatch. But they be all done away wi' now, s'know.'

'Ah, to be sure!'

'Ees, I do mind my mother leadin' me down to the Waterloo veast by the hand, and wi' a younger chile, a little gel, on t'other earm.' . . .

'And what did you have at the feast?'

'Oh, figgy ceake an' tay. Not noo drink – noo beer. I d'low, nor nothen o' that. There was tay an' bread and butter an' ceake. Ees, an' when I wer a bwoy I used to goo along wi' my father and zee the young blackbirds. The gipsies wer there an' wanted a little dog. My father were a tall man – zix veet two inches high, taller nor any other men of the naighbourhood.' . . .

'What was your father? What did he use to do?'

'Do? Oh, anything that come to han'. Often he did beat-plowy. There were scores ov acres all to vuzz, an' they did cut the vuzz and beat-plowy it wi' thease here beat-ploughs.'

'And what have you been?'

'Oh I, I've been a shepherd all my life ever zince I wer zeven year wold. . . . At vust I did pick bits o' ool off hurdles vor to meake mats wi' em. An' I zart ov heckled thissels zometimes. I lived with Mr. Tom Pwope, at Toller, and wer with en aight years. Then I wer ten year doun wi' oone Mr. Stevens doun agean Crewkarne. Lor bless 'ee, I had the best ewes at Appleshaw Fair an' the lambs at Crewkarne. An' I got the lamb prize too. I reared a zight of lambs out ov dree hundred ewes. I've a-bin gooin' dree weeks wi' five hunderd ewes and no maister wi' me all the time, not till show day. . . . They zay that I wer the wonderfullest man in two thousand miles. He, he, he!'

'Quite right. So you are,' exclaimed a sympathetic listener, eyeing the centenarian with due admiration.

'An' ther's nar'a man round here have a-had the schoolin' that I've a had, or can cure the voot rot as I can cure it. When I come up here zome time agoo, an' folk did zay what a mess their sheep wer in wi' the voot rot, I twold 'em what to do. Then I've had 'em wi' the guns or scab vrom head to voot.'

'And what's your special preparation for curing the foot-rot?' I asked. . . . 'A pity to let your secret die with you.'

'No, no, to be zhure,' he observed reflectively. Two moments later he exclaimed decisively, 'Well, I don't mind tellin' you about the stuff – verdigris into about ha'f-a-pint o' sperrits o' zalts – a tay-spoonful. Then a pound o' baccy 'ull meake vower gallons o' stuff vor to cure sheep scab, an' a hogshead o' stuff vor to dip sheep. Ther's nar a man in Darset have ever gone drough the schoolin' that I have, an' can do what I can.' . . .

'You've been married, Job?'

'Oh 'ees, to be zhure. My wife died about twanty year agoo. Her neame were Ann – Ann Samways avore we was marr'd.'

'Have you many children?'

'My wife had seventeen births,' answered the centenarian proudly, with much stress on the number, 'an' I reared I d'think 'tis ten childern, men an' women – nine or ten.' . . .

'Certain London newspapers are anxious to know if you've observed any great changes in the "Hardy Country"?'

'Eh, what? "Hardy Country." Wur's that then? I've a-lived in Darset. Changes? Oh, 'ees. The ground didn't used to be drained zame as 'tis now. There were bogs and pools, vull o' trumpery; but now they be all drained.'

'Did you ever hear of Thomas Hardy?'

'Thomas Hardy? No. What did 'er doo?'

'Write books.'

'Eh, *what* did 'er doo?'

'Write books!' I answered, *crescendo*.

'No. Never yeard o'en.'

If Hardy, despite this minor setback to his reputation, wrote the finest descriptions of Dorset, it was the story of a shepherd which inspired the greatest evocation of Wiltshire life. Strangely and sadly, however, the village upon which much of it was based, Martin on Cranborne Chase, had been transferred to Hampshire by the time that the book was published in 1910. W.H. Hudson, author of A SHEPHERD'S LIFE, lived until his thirties in Argentina, but the last thirty-six years of his life – he died in 1922 – were spent in London. Like Jefferies he turned the eye of the naturalist on to his fellow human beings, here seen enjoying market day in Salisbury.

Before a stall in the market-place a child is standing with her mother – a commonplace-looking, little girl of about twelve, blue-eyed, light-haired, with thin arms and legs, dressed, poorly enough, for her holiday. The mother, stoutish, in her best but much-worn black gown and a brown straw, out-of-shape hat, decorated with bits of ribbon and a few soiled and frayed artificial flowers. Probably she is the wife of a labourer who works hard to keep himself and his family on fourteen shillings a week; and she, too, shows, in her hard hands and sunburnt face, with little wrinkles appearing, that she is a hard worker; but she is very jolly, for she is in Salisbury on market-day, in fine weather, with several shillings in her purse – a shilling for the fares, and perhaps eightpence for refreshments, and the rest to be expended in necessaries for the house. And now to increase the pleasure of the day she has unexpectedly run against a friend! There they stand, the two friends, basket on arm, right in the midst of the jostling crowd, talking in their loud, tinny voices at a tremendous rate; while the girl, with a half-eager, half-listless expression, stands by with her hand on her mother's dress, and every time there is a second's pause in

Melksham, setting off for Bath

Hilperton

the eager talk she gives a little tug at the gown and ejaculates 'Mother!' The woman impatiently shakes off the hand and says sharply: 'What now, Marty! Can't 'ee let me say just a word without bothering!' and on the talk runs again; then another tug and 'Mother!' and then: 'You promised, mother,' and by and by: 'Mother, you said you'd take me to the cathedral next time.'

Having heard so much I wanted to hear more, and addressing the woman I asked her why her child wanted to go. She answered me with a good-humoured laugh: ''Tis all because she heard 'em talking about it last winter, and she'd never been, and I says to her: "Never you mind, Marty, I'll take you there the next time I go to Salisbury."'

'And she's never forgot it,' said the other woman.

'Not she – Marty ain't one to forget.'

'And you been four times, mother,' put in the girl.

'Have I now! Well, 'tis too late now – half-past two, and we must be 't "Goat" at four.'

'Oh, mother, you promised!'

'Well, then, come along, you worriting child, and let's have it over or you'll give me no peace'; and away they went. And I would have followed to know the result if it had been in my power to look into that young brain and see the thoughts and feelings there as the crystal-gazer sees things in a crystal. In a vague way, with some very early memories to help me, I can imagine it – the shock of pleased wonder at the sight of that immense interior, that far-extending nave with pillars that stand like the tall trunks of pines and beeches, and at the end the light screen which allows the eye to travel on through the rich choir, to see, with fresh wonder and delight, high up and far off, that glory of coloured glass as of a window half-open to an unimaginable place beyond – a heavenly cathedral to which all this is but a dim porch or passage! . . .

It was past noon on a hot, brilliant day in August, and that splendid weather had brought in more people than I had ever before seen congregated in Salisbury, and never had the people seemed so talkative and merry and full of life as on that day. I was standing at a busy spot by a row of carriers' carts drawn up at the side of the pavement, just where there are three public-houses close together, when I caught sight of a young man of about twenty-two or twenty-three, a shepherd in a grey suit and thick, iron-shod, old boots and brown leggings, with a soft felt hat thrust jauntily on the back of his head, coming along towards me with that half-slouching, half-swinging gait peculiar to the men of the downs, especially when they are in the town on pleasure bent. Decidedly he was there on pleasure, and had been indulging in a glass or two of beer (perhaps three) and was very happy, trolling out a song in a pleasant, musical voice as he swung along, taking no notice of the people stopping and turning round to stare after him, or of those of his own party who were following and trying to keep up with him, calling to him all the time to stop, to wait, to go slow, and give them a chance. There were seven following him: a stout, middle-aged woman, then a grey-haired old woman and two girls, and last a youngish, married woman with a small boy by the hand; and the stout woman, with a red, laughing face, cried out: 'Oh, Dave, do stop, can't 'ee! Where be going so fast, man – don't 'ee see we can't keep up with 'ee?' But he would not stop nor listen. It was his day out, his great day in Salisbury, a very rare occasion,

and he was very happy. Then she would turn back to the others and cry: ''Tisn't no use, he won't bide for us – did 'ee ever see such a boy!' and laughing and perspiring she would start on after him again. . . .

As he came on I placed myself directly in his path and stared straight into his eyes – grey eyes and very beautiful; but he refused to see me; he stared through me like an animal when you try to catch its eyes, and went by still trolling out his song, with all the others streaming after him.

Shepherding involves not only sheep and shepherds, but also sheep-dogs, and A SHEPHERD'S LIFE is almost as much about dogs as it is about men. Indeed two of the chapters are entitled 'Some sheep-dogs', and 'A sheep-dog's life'. At this sheep-dog trial the dog is found not guilty.

He is a fine old man who has followed a flock these fifty years, and will, I have no doubt, carry his crook for yet

Fovant

another ten. Not only is he a 'good shepherd', . . . with a more intimate knowledge of sheep and all the ailments they are subject to than I have found in any other, but he is also a truly religious man, one that 'walks with God'. He told me this story of a sheep-dog he owned when head-shepherd on a large farm on the Dorsetshire border with a master whose chief delight in life was in coursing hares. They abounded on his land, and he naturally wanted the men employed on the farm to regard them as sacred animals. One day he came out to the shepherd to complain that someone had seen his dog hunting a hare.

The shepherd indignantly asked who had said such a thing.

'Never mind about that,' said the farmer. 'Is it true?'

'It is a lie,' said the shepherd. 'My dog never hunts a hare or anything else. 'Tis my belief the one that said that has got a dog himself that hunts the hares, and he wants to put the blame on someone else.'

'May be so,' said the farmer, unconvinced.

Just then a hare made its appearance, coming across the field directly towards them, and either because they never moved or it did not smell them it came on and on, stopping at intervals to sit for a minute or so on its haunches, then on again until it was within forty yards of where they were standing. The farmer watched it approach and at the same time kept an eye on the dog sitting at their feet and watching the hare too, very steadily. 'Now, shepherd,' said the farmer, 'don't you say one word to the dog and I'll see for myself.' Not a word did he say, and the hare came and sat for some seconds near them, then limped away out of sight, and the dog made not the slightest movement. 'That's all right,' said the farmer, well pleased. 'I know now 'twas a lie I heard about your dog. I've seen for myself and I'll just keep a sharp eye on the man that told me.'

My comment on this story was that the farmer had displayed an almost incredible ignorance of a sheep-dog – and a shepherd. 'How would it have been if you had said, "Catch him, Bob," or whatever his name was?' I asked.

He looked at me with a twinkle in his eye and replied: 'I do b'lieve he'd ha' got 'n, but he'd never move till I told 'n.' . . . When he understood that I was on his side in this question, he told me about a good sheep-dog he once possessed which he had to get rid of because he would not take a hare!

A dog when broken is made to distinguish between the things he must and must not do. He is 'feelingly persuaded' by kind words and caresses in one case and hard words and hard blows in the other. He learns that if he hunts hares and rabbits it will be very bad for him, and in due time, after some suffering, he is able to overcome this strongest instinct of a dog. He acquires an artificial conscience. Then, when his education is finished, he must be made to understand that it is not quite finished after all – that he must partially unlearn one of the saddest of the lessons instilled in him. He must hunt a hare or rabbit when told by his master to do so. It is a compact between man and dog. Thus, they have got a law which the dog has sworn to obey; but the man who made it is above the law and can when he thinks proper command his servant to break it. The dog, as a rule, takes it all in very readily and often allows himself more liberty than his master gives him; the most highly accomplished animal is one that, like my shepherd's dog in the former instance, will not stir till he is told. In the other case the poor brute could not rise to the position; it was too complex for him, and when ordered to catch a rabbit he could only put his tail between his legs and look in a puzzled way at his master. 'Why do you tell me to do a thing for which I shall be thrashed?'

It was only after Caleb had known me some time, when we were fast friends, that he talked with perfect freedom of these things and told me of his own small, illicit takings without excuse or explanation.

In 1906 W.H. Hudson met Edward Thomas, and they became firm friends; indeed Hudson once said that he saw in Thomas the son that he had wanted. Edward Thomas was born in 1878, and between 1899 and his enlistment in the army in 1915 he made a precarious living as a writer and literary critic. He wrote a notable biography of Richard Jefferies, and published several books in the genre which would now be called 'travel-ogues'. He knew Wiltshire well, both from family connections, and from his work on Jefferies, so that his descriptions of the Wessex countryside are informed and perceptive. Here, from his book IN PURSUIT OF SPRING, published in 1914, we find him happy but pensive.

I was looking for Orcheston St. Mary. One sunny February day, when the fields by the road hither from Tilshead were flooded with pools and channels of green, peacock-blue, and purple by the Winterbourne, I had seen below me among the loops of the water a tiny low-towered church with roof stained orange, and a white wall curving and long, and a protective group of elms, which was Orcheston St. Mary. I continued along the stream and its banks of parsley and celandine, its troop of willows, beeches, and elms, but found myself at Orcheston St. George. A cottage near the church bore upon its wall these words, cut in stone, before Queen Victoria's time, –

> Fear God
> Honour the King
> Do good to all men.

Probably it dates from about the year of Alton Work-house, from the times when kites and ravens abounded, and thrived on the corpses of men who were hanged for a little theft committed out of necessity or love of sport. The fear of God must have been a mighty thing to bring forth such laws and still more the obedience to them. And yet, thanks to our capacity for seeing the past and the remote in rose-colour, that age frequently appears as at least a silver age; perhaps even our own will appear German silver. I confess I did not think about the lad who was hanged for a hare when I caught sight of the church at Orcheston St. George, but rather of some imaginary, blissful time which at least lacked our tortures, our great men, our shame and conscience. It is a flint church with an ivied tower standing on terms of equality among thatched farm buildings and elms. The church was stifling, for a stove roared among dead daffodils and moss and the bodies of Ambrose Paradice, gent, dead since 1727, and Joan his wife, and the mere tablet of John Shettler of Elston, who died at Harnham ('from the effects of an accident') on December 6, 1861, when he was fifty-two, and went to Hazelbury Brian in Dorset to be buried. Outside, the sun was almost as warm on the daisies and on the tombstone of Job Gibbs, who died in 1817 at the age of sixty-four, and proclaimed, or the sexton did for him, –

> Ye living men the Tomb survey
> Where you must quickly dwell.
> Mark how the awful summons sounds
> In ev'ry funeral knell.
> Give joy or sorrow, care or pain,
> Take life and friends away,
> But let me find them all again
> In that eternal day.

Close by, Ann Farr from Shropshire, a servant for fifty years at the Rectory, had a tablet between her and oblivion.

The travel writing of Edward Thomas, though more pene-trating, is in some ways reminiscent of Richard Le Gallienne, who told us earlier the tale of the executed vermin. In 1914, drawing on his notebooks of observations, Thomas began to write poetry. He too had observed the country custom of exhibiting the remains of 'various small criminals', as Le Gallienne had called them, and used the motif in his poem, 'The Gallows', composed in 1916.

Army horses on Salisbury Plain

First World War camp, Codford

There was a weasel lived in the sun
With all his family,
Till a keeper shot him with his gun
And hung him up on a tree,
Where he swings in the wind and the rain,
In the sun and in the snow,
Without pleasure, without pain,
On the dead oak tree bough.

There was a crow who was no sleeper,
But a thief and a murderer
Till a very late hour; and this keeper
Made him one of the things that were,
To hang and flap in rain and wind,
In the sun and in the snow.
There are no more sins to be sinned
On the dead oak tree bough.

There was a magpie, too,
Had a long tongue and a long tail;
He could both talk and do –
But what did that avail?
He, too, flaps in the wind and rain
Alongside weasel and crow,
Without pleasure, without pain,
On the dead oak tree bough.

And many other beasts
And birds, skin, bone and feather,
Have been taken from their feasts
And hung up there together,
To swing and have endless leisure
In the sun and in the snow,
Without pain, without pleasure,
On the dead oak tree bough.

The image is charged with the foreboding of a soldier preparing to be sent to the front. In January 1917 Thomas found himself posted to one of the many camps around Salisbury Plain, at Codford in the Wylye Valley. Here are excerpts from the diary which he kept during this period.

20.1.1917

. . . Mild snowy. Arranging stores. Guns arriving. Smith to Bath. So I had to see to unloading and parking the guns till dark. No use walking after dark. The roads are pitch dark and crowded with men going to cinemas, darkness worse from blaze of motor lamps and electric light in camps nearby. Long queues waiting outside cinema at 5.30. Tested battery compass. Talk with Fenner about martens in Ireland, badgers, plovers, barrows etc.

21.1.1917

No church parade for me. 9.30–1.30 walked over Stockton Down, the Bake, and under Grovely Wood to Barford St Martin, Burcombe, and to lunch at Netherhampton House with Newbolts. Freezing drizzle – freezes on ground, white grass and icy roads. 2 families of vagrants in green road roasting a corpse of something by slow wood fire. Beautiful Downs, with one or two isolated thatched barns, ivied ash trees, and derelict threshing machines. Old milestones lichened as with battered gold and silver nails. Back by train at 5. Tea alone. Guns in line out on parade square. Smith back. Letter from Helen, Ingpen, Eleanor, Hudson. Letter to Helen, Ingpen. Talk with Fenner after dinner about fishing – river and sea. . . .

27.1.1917

A clear windy frosty dawn, the sun like a bright coin between the knuckles of opposite hills seen from sidelong. A fox. A little office work. Telegram to say Baba was at Ransome's, so I walked over Downs by Chicklade Bottom and the Fonthills to Hatch, and blistered both feet badly. House full of ice and big fires. Sat up with Ivy till 12 and slept till 8. Another fine bright frosty day on the –

28.1.1917

Wrote to Bronwen, Helen, Ivy, Eleanor. Letters from Bronwen, Helen, Mother, Eleanor. Slept late. Rested my feet, talking to the children or Ivy cooking with Kitty Gurd. Hired a bicycle to save walking. Such a beautiful ride after joining the Mere and Amesbury Road at Fonthill Bishop – hedgeless roads over long sloping downs with woods and sprinkled thorns, carved with old tracks which junipers line – an owl and many rabbits – a clear pale sky and but a faint sunset – a long twilight lasting till 6. We are to move at 6.30 a.m. tomorrow. . . .

Nine weeks later Edward Thomas was killed at the Battle of Arras.

But we must not end on a sombre note. Instead let us go back a few years, and share with Hudson the glory of a Wessex sunset.

When the mackerel visit the coast, and come near enough to be taken in a draw-net, every villager who owns a share (usually a tenth) in a fishing-boat throws down his spade or whatever implement he happens to have in his hand at the moment, and hurries away to the beach to take his share in the fascinating task. At four o'clock one morning a youth, who had been down to the sea to watch, came running into the village uttering loud cries which were like excited yells – a sound to rouse the deepest sleeper. The mackerel had come! For the rest of the day there was a pretty kind of straggling procession of those who went and came between the beach and the village – men in blue cotton shirts, blue jerseys, blue jackets, and women in grey gowns and big white sun-bonnets. During the latter part of the day the proceedings were peculiarly interesting to me, a looker-on with no share in any one of the boats, owing to the catches being composed chiefly of jelly-fish. Some sympathy was felt for the toilers who strained their muscles again and again only to be mocked in the end; still, a draught of jelly-fish was

more to my taste than one of mackerel. The great weight of a catch of this kind when the net was full was almost too much for the ten or twelve men engaged in drawing it up; then (to the sound of deep curses from those of the men who were not religious) the net would be opened and the great crystalline hemispheres, hyaline blue and delicate salmon-pink in colour, would slide back into the water. Such rare and exquisite colours have these great glassy flowers of ocean that to see them was a feast; and every time a net was hauled up my prayer – which I was careful not to repeat aloud – was, Heaven send another big draught of jelly-fish!

The sun, sinking over the hills towards Swyre and Bridport, turned crimson before it touched the horizon. The sky became luminous; the yellow Chesil Bank, stretching long leagues away, and the hills behind it, changed their colours to violet. The rough sea near the beach glittered like gold; the deep green water, flecked with foam, was mingled with fire; the one boat that remained on it, tossing up and down near the beach, was like a boat of ebony in a glittering fiery sea. A dozen men were drawing up the last net; but when they gathered round to see what they had taken – mackerel or jelly-fish – I cared no longer to look with them. That sudden, wonderful glory which had fallen on the earth and sea had smitten me as well and changed me; and I was like some needy homeless tramp who has found a shilling piece, and, even while he is gloating over it, all at once sees a great treasure before him – glittering gold in heaps, and all rarest sparkling gems, more than he can gather up.

But it is a poor simile. No treasures in gold and gems, though heaped waist-high all about, could produce in the greediest man, hungry for earthly pleasures, a delight, a rapture, equal to mine. For this joy was of another and higher order and very rare, and was a sense of lightness and freedom from all trammels as if the body had become air, essence, energy, or soul, and of union with all visible

Sutton Poyntz

Lulworth Cove

nature, one with sea and land and the entire vast over-arching sky. . . .

The glory passed and with it the exaltation: the earth and sea turned grey; the last boat was drawn up on the slope and the men departed slowly: only one remained, a rough-looking youth, about fifteen years old. Some important matter which he was revolving in his mind had detained him alone on the darkening beach. He sat down, then stood up and gazed at the sea rolling wave after wave to roar and hiss on the shingle at his feet; then he moved restlessly about, crunching the pebbles beneath his thick boots; finally, making up his mind, he took off his coat, threw it down, and rolled up his shirt-sleeves, with the resolute air of a man about to engage in a fight with an adversary nearly as big as himself. Stepping back a little space, he made a rush at the sea, not to cast himself in it, but only, as it turned out, with the object of catching some water in the hollow of his hands from the top of an incoming wave. He only succeeded in getting his legs wet, and in hastily retreating he fell on his back. Nothing daunted, he got up and renewed the assault, and when he succeeded in catching water in his hands he dashed it on and vigorously rubbed it over his dirty face. After repeating the operation about a dozen times, receiving meanwhile several falls and wettings, he appeared satisfied, put on his coat and marched away homewards with a composed air.

Chesil

Stalbridge

Bibliography

Ashley, Sir Francis; *The Case Book of Sir Francis Ashley, JP, Recorder of Dorchester, 1614–35*, edited by J.H. Bettey, 1981.

Asser; *Old English Chronicles*, edited by J.A. Giles, 1910.

Aubrey, John; *Brief Lives*, edited by Andrew Clark, 2 vols. 1898.

Aubrey, John; *The Natural History of Wiltshire*, edited by John Britton, 1847.

Aubrey, John; *Three Prose Works*, edited by John Buchanan-Brown, 1972.

Aubrey, John; *Wiltshire: the Topographical Collections*, edited by John Edward Jackson, 1862.

Austen, Jane; *Jane Austen's Letters to her sister Cassandra and others*, edited by R.W. Chapman, 2nd ed. 1952.

Barnes, William; *Poems of rural life in the Dorset dialect*, 1879.

Barrington, Shute; *Wiltshire Returns to the Bishop's Visitation Queries, 1783*, edited by Mary Ransome, 1972.

Black's Guide to Dorsetshire, 1875.

Blake, Malachi; in 'Blandford in 1731' by F.S. Hinchy, *Dorset Year Book*, 1965–6, pp. 145–7.

Britton, John; *The Autobiography of John Britton*, 1850.

Caird, Sir James; *English Agriculture in 1850–51*, 1852.

Camden, William; *Camden's Britannia*, translated by Edmund Gibson, 1695.

Chandler, John; *The Register of John Chandler, Dean of Salisbury, 1404–17*, edited by T.C.B. Timmins, 1984.

Cobbett, William; *Rural Rides* . . . , 1830.

Defoe, Daniel; *A Tour through the whole Island of Great Britain*, 1724–6.

Drayton, Michael; *Poly-Olbion*, 1933.

Eden, Sir Frederic Morton; *The State of the Poor* . . . , vol. 3, 1797.

Eulogium (Historiarum sive Temporis) . . . , vol. 1, edited by F.S. Haydon, 1858.

Fiennes, Celia; *The Illustrated Journeys of Celia Fiennes*, 1982.

Fuller, Thomas; *The Worthies of England*, 1952.

Geoffrey of Monmouth; *Old English Chronicles*, edited by J.A. Giles, 1910.

Gilpin, William; *Observations on the Western Parts of England, relative chiefly to Picturesque Beauty* . . . , 1798.

Ham, Elizabeth, *Elizabeth Ham by herself*, edited by Eric Gillett, 1945.

Hardy, Thomas; *The Return of the Native*, 1878.

Hardy, Thomas; *Tess of the D'Urbervilles*, 1891.

Hardy, Thomas; *The Trumpet Major*, 1880.

Hare, Augustus J.C.; *Memorials of a Quiet Life*, 11th ed., 2 vols. 1874.

Hudson, William Henry; *Afoot in England*, 1909.

Hudson, William Henry; *A Shepherd's Life*, 1910.

Hunt, Henry; *Memoirs of Henry Hunt, Esq. written by himself*, 2 vols. 1820.

Ivie, John; *Poverty in Early Stuart Salisbury*, edited by Paul Slack, 1975.

Jefferies, Richard; *The Story of my Heart*, 1883.

Jefferies, Richard; *Wild Life in a Southern County*, 1879.

Kilvert, Francis; *Kilvert's Diary, 1870–1879*, edited by William Plomer, 3 vols. 1938–40.

King, W.H.; 'A Tale of 70 Years Ago', *Dorset Year Book*, 1945–6, p. 153.

Le Gallienne, Richard; *Travels in England*, 1900.

Leland, John; *The Itinerary of John Leland* . . . , edited by Lucy Toulmin Smith, 5 vols. 1907–10.

Lipscomb, George; *A Journey into Cornwall* . . . , 1799.

March, H. Colley; 'The Giant and the Maypole of Cerne', *Proceedings of the Dorset Natural History and Antiquarian Field Club*, vol. 22, 1901, pp. 101–18.

Maton, William George; *Observations relative chiefly to the Natural History . . . of the Western Counties of England*, 2 vols. 1797.

Nova Legenda Anglie . . . , vol. 2 edited by Carl Horstmann, 1901.

Pouncy, Harry; 'The Centenarian Speaks: Memories of a Veteran Dorset Shepherd', *The Society of Dorset Men in London*, 1910–11, pp. 97–100.

Primrose, Deborah; *A Modern Boeotia: Pictures from Life in a Country Parish*, 1904.

Smith, Sydney; *The Letters of Sydney Smith*, edited by Nowell C. Smith, 2 vols. 1953.

Thomas, Edward; *The Collected Poems of Edward Thomas*, edited by R. George Thomas, 1981.

Thomas, Edward; *In Pursuit of Spring*, 1914.

Whiteway, William; 'The Commonplace Book of a Dorsetshire Man (AD 1625–1635)' by W.M. Barnes, *Proceedings of the Dorset Natural History and Antiquarian Field Club*, vol. 16, 1895, pp. 59–74.

Williams, Alfred; *A Wiltshire Village*, 1912.

Worcestre, William; *William Worcestre Itineraries*, edited by John H. Harvey, 1969.

Index

This is a selective index to places, persons and book titles mentioned in the text.

Acknowledgements

I should like to thank the following for allowing me to quote from copyright material: Clarendon Press (letters of Sydney Smith); Messrs Faber and Faber (Elizabeth Ham); Dr J.H. Bettey (Sir Francis Ashley); Oxford University Press (diary of Edward Thomas, Jane Austen); Wiltshire Record Society (Shute Barrington, John Chandler, John Ivie); Messrs Webb and Bower (Celia Fiennes). I am most grateful to the photographers whose work is included in this book: Tim Hawkins, David Tavener, Michael Dunsby, Alison Borthwick, Derek Irvine, Michael Taylor and Stuart Whale. For help in various ways I wish to thank also: Michael Marshman, Felicity Gilmour and the staff of Wiltshire County Council Library and Museum Service at Devizes, Salisbury and Trowbridge; Ken Rogers and the staff of the Wiltshire Record Office; the staffs of Dorchester Reference Library (Dorset County Library), Bath Reference Library (Avon County Library), Southampton University Library and the University of London Library; Mr Fred Langford of the Society of Dorset Men; Alan Sutton, Jaqueline Mitchell and Roger Thorp of Alan Sutton Publishing; Dave Cousins, Fay and Patrick Dillon, Eric Jones, and especially my wife, Alison Borthwick, for unfailing help and interest.

The credits and information on all illustrations used in this book are given in page ascending sequence. In the case of colour illustrations (which all date from the period 1976–90) the source refers to the photographer (MD = Michael Dunsby; TH = Tim Hawkins; DT = David Tavener). Most sepia-reproduced photographs date from the period 1890–1920, and are in the possession of the author (JHC) or Wiltshire County Council Library and Museum Service (WLMS). Sources of line illustrations are abbreviated as follows: AW, *Ancient Wiltshire* by Sir Richard Colt Hoare (vol. 2, 1821); BW, *The Beauties of Wiltshire* by John Britton (3 vols, 1801, 1825); HACD, *The History and Antiquities of the County of Dorset* by John Hutchins (3rd ed., 1861–73); IC, *Itinerarium Curiosum* by William Stukeley (1776 ed.); JBA *John Britton's Autobiography* (1850); PDNHAS, *Proceedings of the Dorset Natural History and Archaeological Society*; PMS, *Picturesque Memorials of Salisbury*, by Peter Hall (1834).

Page **2** The Square, Corfe Castle, *JHC*; **3** Burton Bradstock, *JHC*; **6** Westbury White Horse, *JHC*; **8** Salisbury Plain, *TH*; **9** Stonehenge, from J. Webb, *A Vindication of Ston'heng Restored*, 1665; **11** Cromlech at Portesham, *HACD*; **12** Devil's Den, Preshute, *JHC*; **14** Malmesbury Abbey, from J. Moffat, *A History of Malmesbury*; **16** River Kennet, Axford, *MD*; **17** Salisbury, *JHC*; **19** Portland, *JHC*; **20** Limpley Stoke, *DT*; **21** Chesil, looking east from Bridport, *TH*; **22** Lyme Regis (from a postcard), *JHC*; **23** detail from J. Ogilby, *Britannia*, 1675; **24** Portland Bill, *TH*; **25** The Purbeck Hills, *TH*; **26** Plan of Portland, 1710, *HACD*; **27** Corfe Castle, *HACD*; **28** Corfe, *TH*; **29** Prospect of Poole, *HACD*; **31** Portland, from Abbotsbury Hill, *TH*; **32** Salisbury Cathedral, *WLMS*; **33** Lyme Regis, *IC*; **34** Stair Hole, *TH*; **36** Symondsbury, *HACD*; **37** Enford, *JHC*; **38** Gold Hill, Shaftesbury, *TH*; **41** Corsley, *JHC*; **42** Mere, from Castle Hill, *JHC*; **43** View of Salisbury, *PMS*; **45** Fiddleford Mill, The Stour, *TH*; **46** Salisbury, The Council House, *PMS*; **47** Brass of Sir John Tregonwell, *PDNHAS*, vol. 28, 1907; **48** Broad Chalke, *Stuart Whale*; **49** John Aubrey, from J. Aubrey and J.E. Jackson, *Wiltshire Collections*, 1862; **50** Downs to the north of the Vale of Pewsey, *TH*; **51** Lacock, *DT*; **52** Lacock Abbey, *BW*; **54** Avebury, *DT*; **55** Wilton House, *BW*; **56** Corsham, *WLMS*; **57** Off for a jaunt, *JHC*; **58** West Kennett, from the Sanctuary, from W. Stukeley, *Abury*, 1743; **59** Marlborough, *IC*; **60** Amesbury, *JHC*; **61** Devizes Market-Place, *WLMS*; **62** Silbury Hill, *AW*; **63** Brownsea Castle, *HACD*; **64** Lyme Regis, *JHC*; **65** Whitchurch Canonicorum, *JHC*; **66** Merly House, *HACD*; **67** Poole Harbour, *TH*; **68** Lulworth Cove, *HACD*; **70** Milton Abbas, *TH*; **71** Stourhead, *DT*; **72** Dorchester, *IC*; **73** Water-mill near Lyme Regis, *JHC*; **74** West Bay, Bridport, *TH*; **76** Shrewton, *JHC*; **77** Aldbourne, *WLMS*; **79** Chesil, *TH*; **80** Chippenham bridge, *BW*; **82** Blackmoor Vale, *TH*; **84** The Great Bustard, from *Wiltshire Archaeological and Natural History Magazine*, vol. 3, 1857; **86** Rawlsbury Camp, Bulbarrow Hill, *TH*; **87** View of Blackmoor Vale, from Shaftesbury, *TH*; **88** Blandford Forum, old church, *HACD*; **89** Blandford Forum, new church, *HACD*; **90** River Cerne, with Nether Cerne behind, *TH*; **91** Watercress beds, Broad Chalke, *Derek Irvine*; **92** Castle Combe, *JHC*; **94** Cherhill, *MD*; **95** The River Piddle, near Throop, *TH*; **96** Wiltshire cottage interior, *JBA*; **97** Fox in cradle, *JBA*; **98** Sherborne, *JHC*; **99** North Bradley, *WLMS*; **103** Chapmanslade, *JHC*; **104** Portland, *TH*; **105** Chiswell, Portland, *TH*; **106** Lyme Regis, *JHC*; **108** Golden Cap, *TH*; **109** Near Kimmeridge Bay, *TH*; **111** Weymouth, *JHC*; **113** Looking west to Portland from Flower's Barrow fort, *TH*; **114** Swanage, *JHC*; **115** Eype, *JHC*; **118** Weymouth Sands, *JHC*; **119** The Crown, Everleigh, *JHC*; **121** Marlborough Downs, *TH*; **124** The Marlborough Downs, near Rockley, *MD*; **125** Stubble burning, Little Bedwyn, *MD*; **127** Alton Barnes, *JHC*; **129** Kington St Michael, *JBA*; **130** Dorset village shop, *JHC*; **131** Mere, *WLMS*; **132** Model farm, Longleat, from S. Copland, *Agriculture ancient and modern*, vol. 2, 1866; **134** Shaftesbury, *JHC*; **135** Milton Abbas, *JHC*; **138** Biddestone, *JHC*; **140** The bridge, Bradford on Avon, *DT*; **141** Sandy Lane, *DT*; **144** Maiden Castle, *TH*; **146** Gold Hill, Shaftesbury, *JHC*; **147** Winterbourne Dauntsey, *JHC*; **148** Dorcester, engraving by William Barnes, *PDNHAS*, vol. 46, 1925; **149** William Barnes, *PDNHAS*, vol. 26, 1905; **150** Declaring the poll, Swindon, 1910, *JHC*; **151** Oare, *DT*; **152** Trackway over St Anne's Hill, *AW*; **155** Box Valley, *Alison Borthwick*; **159** Stonehenge, *Michael Taylor*; **163** Trying to keep still, *JHC*; **166** Flamstone, near Bishopstone, *WLMS*; **167** Tilshead, *JHC*; **169** Abbotsbury, *JHC*; **170** The River Stour, near Sturminster, *TH*; **173** Melksham, setting off for Bath, *WLMS*; **174** Hilperton, *DT*; **175** Wiltshire ram, from T. Davis, *General view of the agriculture of Wiltshire*, 1811; **176** Shepherd and sheep-dog, by B.C. Gotch, from W.H. Hudson, *A Shepherd's Life*, 1910; **177** Fovant, *JHC*; **180** Army horses on Salisbury Plain, *JHC*; **181** First World War camp, Codford, *JHC*; **184** Sutton Poyntz, *JHC*; **185** Lulworth Cove, *JHC*; **187** Chesil, *TH*; **188** Stalbridge, *JHC*.

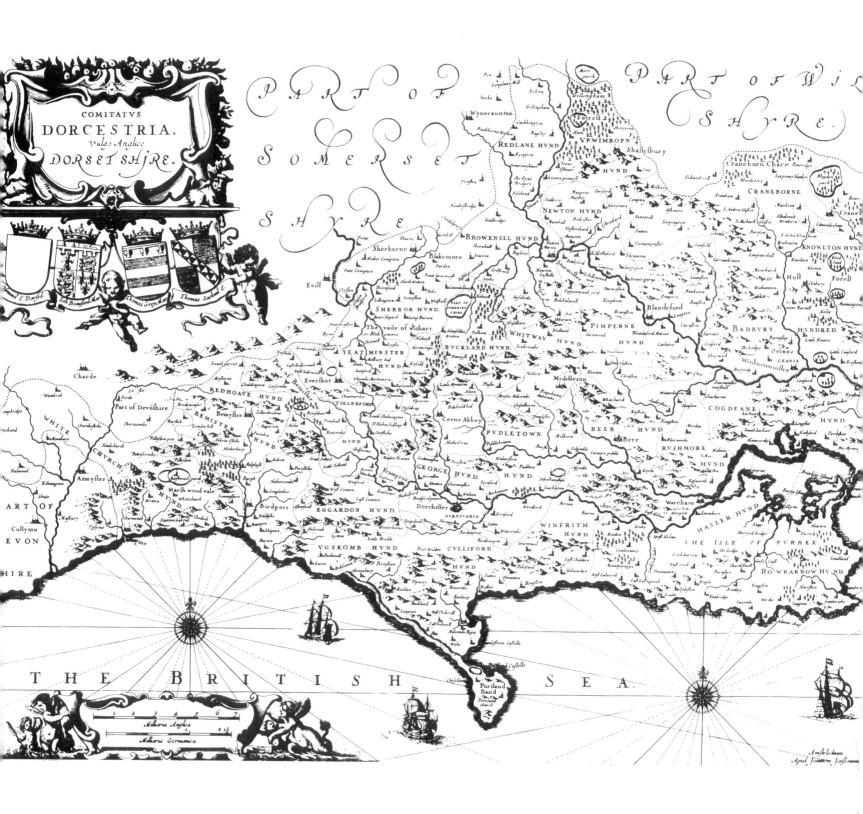